ADVANCE PRAISE
Who Peed On My Yoga Mat?

⚜

"Lela Davidson's stories are so heartwarming and hilarious, you'll feel like she's your best friend and wish she was your neighbor. Her essays are like eating carbs, the more you have, the more you want."

Robin O'Bryant, author of *Ketchup is a Vegetable and Other Lies Moms Tell Themselves*

"Lela Davidson is fifty shades of hilarious. After reading this book, you'll never look at your yoga mat or shower scrubber the same way again."

Jenna McCarthy, author of *If It Was Easy, They'd Call the Whole Damn Thing a Honeymoon: Living with and Loving the TV-Addicted, Sex-Obsessed, Not-So-Handy Man You Married*

"She might have been 'Blacklisted from the PTA,' but I LOVE Lela Davidson! With her irreverent approach to parenting and wicked sense of humor, she's the hilarious bad mother you'll want for your best friend."

Tracy Beckerman, syndicated humor columnist and author of *Lost in Suburbia: A Momoir: How I Got Pregnant, Lost Myself, And Got My Cool Back in the New Jersey Suburbs.*

"The laughs don't stop in Lela Davidson's new book of essays *Who Peed on My Yoga Mat?*. You can read the single serve essays when you only have a few minutes to be entertained, but you can't just read one! You want to read them one after the other because they're that good and that engaging. It's the crack cocaine of parenting humor. And what a voice she has! When you read Davidson's words you'll feel as if she's right there reading to you. So don't keep it in the bathroom. And don't pee on Lela Davidson's yoga mat. She doesn't like that."

Eric Ruhalter, author of *The Kid Dictionary: Hilarious Words to Describe the Indescribable Things Kids Do*

"Reading Lela's Davidson's stories about middle American motherhood is like having the good luck to sit next to someone at the soccer meet or school fundraiser who turns out to be wickedly smart, unexpectedly subversive and terribly funny. You just know you will be friends."

Kyran Pittman, author of *Planting Dandelions: Field Notes on a Semi-Domesticated Life*

"Self-effacing, witty and insightful—loved it! We can all relate to the "am I doing this wrong?" feeling in Lela's writing. She's like the coolest, funniest mom you could hope to sit next to at the playground."

Diane Mizota, host of Yahoo Shine's *Away We Grow*

"Lela Davidson is smart, witty, and brazenly candid. Reading this book induced a potpourri of reactions from knowing nods, to incredulous shock, to drink through my nose laughter. Davidson explores the quirks of everyday life as a mother, wife, and independent woman. Through candor and self-deprecating prose she shows us how to find humor and joy in almost any situation."

Rob Sachs, author of *What Would Rob Do?: An Irreverent Guide to Surviving Life's Daily Indignities*

Who Peed on My Yoga Mat?

more stories from
a perfectly imperfect life

LELA DAVIDSON

Author of the award-winning collection BLACKLISTED FROM THE PTA

JUPITER PRESS

Who Peed on My Yoga Mat?
by Lela Davidson

ISBN: 978-1-936214-96-9

Library of Congress Control Number: 2012946360

Author Photo by Sweet Portrayal Photography, www.sweetportrayal.com

Published by Jupiter Press, imprint of Wyatt-MacKenzie

JUPITER PRESS

jupiterpress@wyattmackenzie.com

LELA DAVIDSON

For John, Alexander, and Gabriella, my favorite people
in the whole wide world.

LELA DAVIDSON

A Note to the New PTA

Dear PTA,

The backpacks are still relatively fresh and the air retains a tinge of that new school smell, but before we go any further into the chalk and Goldfish wonderland that is the school year, there are a few things you should know about me.

I spend countless hours devoted to the care, feeding, and moral development of my children during their non-school hours. Therefore I am reluctant to sign on for any of your clipboard-worthy activities. They're just so... time-consuming. Frankly, I've put in my time as Cheerful Mommy, so unless you're recruiting for chaperones to accompany students abroad, expect me to become suddenly engrossed in my Twitter feed while the sign-up sheet is passed.

That said, I am a surprisingly dutiful worker bee. That's right, after you ask me just four or five times I will happily agree to work a shift or bake a cake or whatever else chips away at the greater good. I will show up with a smile and I won't spend the entire time talking smack about the other PTA parents. Except for Visible Thong Mom. She's fair game.

Regarding fundraisers, I will wholeheartedly support the projects I like, as well as anything that gives me an excuse to drink too much and get my picture taken in a nice dress. On the other hand, I will fight like a mother against anything

I feel is immoral or unethical that is being conducted in my child's name. So please, for the love of frozen cookie dough, let's agree not to go door-to-door with ammunition, crack, or sexual favors—not even the pretend kind. Furthermore, I don't do yogurt lids, aluminum can tabs, or box tops. This is non-negotiable.

You should also know that except for the aforementioned semester in Paris, I can't volunteer for any jobs with the words "field" or "monitor" in the description. These invariably involve other people's children. Here's the thing: I don't like them. There are only a few humans under the age of twenty I'm actually fond of: The ones that emerged from a large incision in my abdomen, a handful of their friends, and their better-behaved cousins. Believe me, I'm doing us all a favor by declining any student-related duties up front. Kids never believe my "I'll smack you in the head" threats until it's too late. No one wants that lawsuit. Plus, most of them are bigger than me now and asking for a step stool diminishes my authority.

Finally, be ye informed that I wrote a book called *Black-listed from the PTA*, in which I encourage other moms to do whatever it takes to get banned from the PTA. Forever.

But it was a joke. A true joke. Okay, fine, a manifesto of sorts.

I pinky promise not to undermine any of your future efforts. Honestly, PTA, it's nothing personal. Some of my best friends are Queen Bees in your fine organization. So keep those guilt-inducing emails coming. I'll respond, I'll sign your clipboard. I'll do my part. Eventually.

Sincerely,
That Blacklisted Mom

LELA DAVIDSON

TABLE OF CONTENTS

❧

Adventures & Advice

Life on the Cul-de-Sac

Marital Bliss

The Making
of a Mom

Of Babies and Carpet

W HEN MY HUSBAND AND I BECAME PARENTS, we were living the good life on Seattle's fashionable Queen Anne Hill. Our condo was in a brand new building with a bus stop outside and a coffee shop on the ground level. We walked to the grocery store, gym, and free concerts under the Space Needle. The spotless dwelling had been the ideal place to enjoy the short-lived double-income-no-kids phase of our lives together. At nine hundred square feet, the two-bedroom apartment felt roomy, even after we put up the crib and created parking spaces for the strollers. (You can't have just one.) The convenient location made even more sense once we were a family. Within walking distance were our son's pediatrician, several parks, and friends who didn't flinch at a little vomit on the sofa.

It was perfect.

Naturally, we had to move.

Much as we loved the six-square-foot lanai, it wasn't a yard. A child needs to crawl in the grass and chase butterflies. Getting lost in the alfalfa sprout section of Trader Joe's would not suffice. That is why, about the time my son's umbilical cord fell off, we decided to abandon urban life, cash in on the condo, with its still new-smelling white carpet, and move to a real house with a real lawn. We hoped for the next hill over. Magnolia, with its views, grass, and blackberries, was a coveted destination where we could really settle into family life.

"Are you sure?" everyone asked. "Won't that be kind of stressful? Selling your place and moving with a new baby?"

Pfft. Stressful. What was stressful was the thought that the Peter Rabbit border in the nursery would be our son's only connection to the natural world. I ignored the advice of well-meaning friends and attached myself to the online MLS service where I soon found many suitable homes in our target neighborhood, including The One. The One had wood floors (under the carpet), thick moldings, and an incredible yard full of mature hydrangeas, roses, viburnum, and a camellia hedge.

This was 1998, before the dot-com crash. Seattle's real estate values soared with the stock prices of Microsoft and Amazon. Our condo was worth at least twenty percent more than what we'd paid 18 months prior. Unfortunately, the homes we wanted to buy were listed at peak prices too. My first pick, with the super special yard, was the most expensive of our options. At $240,000, the two-bedroom, one-bath house was slightly out of our price range, but we couldn't pass up the chance to spend every weekend knee deep in weeds and grass clippings in one of the best neighborhoods in the city.

Not to mention the sprawling 1,100 square feet.

The realtor assured us that as the only new construction in an established neighborhood, our condo was in demand. Still, the timing had to be just right. If we didn't sell it quickly, someone else was going to be clipping my lilacs and pruning my roses.

We immediately placed a contingent offer and set out to stage the condo for sale. No off-putting personal photos on the mantle, no weird baby food residue in the sink, and I had to vacate immediately whenever someone wanted to see the place. Because I was still home on maternity leave, I planned to make my quick exits to the coffee shop downstairs. After a slight learning curve I could pack myself, my baby, and a fully stocked diaper bag in under five minutes. Not bad for a newbie.

Raising babies, selling real estate. What stress?

A few days into the process I received a call from the realtor and commenced my routine. I gathered my son's things and set him on the changing table for a fresh diaper before heading downstairs where I'd order a latte and settle my son in for some under-the-receiving blanket nursing. I felt lucky, certain that today was the day my condo would sell itself.

Motherhood: Check. Selling condos: Ace!

No sooner had I removed my son's diaper than a stunning display of nature's bounty escaped him. Nearly fluorescent in color, propelled through the air by the mighty force of my infant's tiny bowel, came a great arch of liquid shit. I was mesmerized, but only for a moment—until I realized that the impressive fountain of excrement was headed straight for the white carpet. Before I could act, the stench hit me. (Whoever said breastfed babies' poop doesn't stink was full of breastfed babies' poop.) My maternal reflexes were quick, if not so maternal. With the table, baby, and floor full of mustardy muck, I abandoned my son on the changing table in quest of the spot remover.

Don't judge me. We had escrow at stake. I sprayed, dabbed, and scrubbed, but the yellow ring of shame remained. I felt less lucky as I wiped down the furniture. I rinsed the boy in the bathroom sink.

But the showing must go on.

The scent of Newborn Ass lingered in the air as I hurried downstairs. Maybe no one would notice. My latte did not taste right and my baby boy would not latch on.

We did not receive an offer that day. However, I developed valuable expertise in untimely blowout management and stain removal. We ended up selling our condo in time to snatch up the happy yard home, closing on a brisk afternoon just before Thanksgiving.

An hour after the realtor handed us the keys to our new house, we ripped out the carpet—just in case the previous owners ever had a baby.

LELA DAVIDSON

Potty Training, Over-Achiever Style

ON FRIDAY MY FRIEND TOLD ME she was staying in all week-end to potty train her 18-month-old daughter. Because, as we all know, the only thing more disgraceful than a snotty toddler is a shitty one. By Monday this formerly rational woman had chronicled the sequestered potty training adventure on her blog. To facilitate her daughter's successful transition to regular toileting, she remained in the house for a period measured in days, launching a full-blown campaign. There was decor. And a theme: polka dots. She thought of every detail, M&Ms, a festively wrapped pee-pee-in-the-potty-prize, and to record the special deposits on the calendar, garage sale pricing stickers. Polka dots. Her plan fell just short of hiring a polka-dotted clown.

But the grand finale.

Are you ready?

When the child finally goes poo-poo in the potty, she's getting an iPod. In a stark contrast that says much about my own parenting philosophy—or lack thereof—my kid had a book and a video with a song that I still can't get out of my head.

> *Yes, I'm going to the potty, potty.*
> *Yes, I'm going to the potty, potty.*
> *Yes, I'm going to the potty potty, now-ow!*
> *[bass solo]*

My friend—the Potty Impresario, the Commander of the Commode, the Headmistress of the Head—is not a nut job. She reads books, works in electronic commerce, and maintains functional relationships with other adults who regularly use the bathroom. And yet, this typically rational woman seemed consumed by the drive to potty train her daughter. Perhaps the proliferation of blogs and social bookmarking inspired some of the craftiness, incentives, and tracking devices she employed to get her child to piss in a pot, but technology is not the root cause of her temporary insanity.

This woman is at a vulnerable place in first-time motherhood. Everything feels significant and everyone has an opinion. I imagine at least a dozen women at her office/church/block party/play group who brag relentlessly about the age at which their own first born children potty-trained/recited a psalm/calibrated the hatches on the international space station. This good-natured conceit can make a new mother feel like she is failing at the most important thing in the whole world, which is of course, nurturing a kid who is just as good—oh, who are we kidding, *better than*—everybody else's kid.

If only she would quit shitting her pants.

We have all been there. We over-achievers, that is.

When my son was eighteen months old, I too worried he'd never squat in the right place. I just couldn't get excited about how to fix that. Experienced mothers told me not to worry.

"No one ever left for college with a diaper on," they said.

I doubt that can be proven, but even if it's true, the logic is flawed and irrelevant.

A kid who pees in the Kindergarten circle before nap time won't make any friends. And without friends, he's not showing up to all those extra-curricular activities so important on college applications. Without those opportunities to build self-esteem, he won't be motivated to study. Pretty soon he's smoking a joint behind the trees, while his early-onset potty-trained peers ace the SATs.

So, sure, he might not be wearing a diaper at eighteen, but he's not leaving for college either.

There is no scrapbook page or blog post recording the potty training of my son. There are no photographic images or video footage of the techniques I used to talk that kid into using the toilet. We have only the tattered copy of the potty book with its adorable cartoon boy bending over to show us where number two comes from. All I know for sure is that by the time my son was two we were hauling a porta-potty up and down I-5 on the 90-minute drives from our home in Seattle to visit the grandparents in Bellingham, stopping on the side of the highway so he could sit on his potty and go.

Regarding this critical milestone for my daughter, there is nothing to remember. She is twenty-two months younger than my son, so by the time it was her turn to potty train, I had abandoned some of my competitive edge. Plus, with two children under four years old, diapers were more convenient than babysitting a toddler's butt. She was just past her second birthday when my son's preschool teacher said she was excited to have Gaby in her class next year.

Except she didn't qualify.

"Don't they have to be potty trained to be in your class?" I asked.

"It's okay," the teacher said. "I'll potty train her."

You'll what?

The light shone on this angel and her promise of the blessed gift.

And damn if she didn't do it. Within a week of starting Big Girl School, Gaby was standing in line for the potty with all her friends. Some children will thrive with prizes and motivational mobiles over the toilet, but the competitive ones are just like us. All it takes is a little peer pressure: Line them up with a group of their equals and the one with wet pants loses.

Tomboys and Tiaras

I WAS CLEANING MY DAUGHTER'S ROOM when the guilt hit. There, among the collection of sports trophies and funky crafts, I began to worry I hadn't properly celebrated the little girl she had been. There were hockey helmets, pictures of silly faces and nature walks, but no evidence of ruffles in sight.

Usually, I'm thrilled that Gaby is more tomboy than tiara. Who can blame her? I think it's in her DNA. As a kid, I didn't match barrettes to shoelaces either. I grew up to wear jeans and suits, the bare minimum of pink, and rarely wore more jewelry than a pair of simple earrings.

Yet sometimes, when I see a picture of an ultra feminine girl, I regret not imbuing my daughter's childhood with more feminine magic. When she was a baby, I dressed Gaby in her brother's hand-me-down overalls and hunter green cords partly because of things like mortgages and electric bills. My son was still in diapers and I didn't have the energy to coordinate outfits. I could have opted for the *stick-a-flower-on-your-baby's head* look, but deemed it unwise to introduce

Karo syrup to a baby with hair.

Cheap, lazy, and wise though I was, my daughter's early childhood was not completely lacking in feminine fashion. Not long after she learned to walk, I bought her the most beautiful shoes, white with tiny hand-sewn leather flowers. She wore them to church for a whole year. That was approximately three times. Add to that a couple of brunches. For a seventy-five dollar pair of shoes, that worked out to fifteen dollars a wearing, not exactly cost effective, but every time I saw her little feet in those shoes I melted.

I'd like to think I protected her from the fairy tale fantasy, waiting around in some tower for Prince Charming to come along so she could start her life. And I'm beyond grateful she never emulated those inappropriately fetching Disney princesses. But I still wonder if I should have decked Gaby out in buttons and bows when she was a baby.

When she was five, Gaby joined the cult of dance class, but she wasn't a fan. Her independent spirit rebelled against the structure, and the tomboy in her detested the frilly, shiny costumes. And then there was the eye shadow. The day of the class portrait we arrived at the studio to find all the girls in full foundation, liquid eyeliner, and Technicolor blush. My fresh-faced Kindergartener looked out of place, so I slid some clear lip gloss on her and shoved her into the frame. Not my finest moment, pushing cosmetics on a girl who would sooner dissect worms than play in my makeup drawer.

Then I turned forty and wore a tiara for an entire month. I wore it everywhere—to parties, to board meetings, and nightclubs. I sparkled at an Oklahoma truck stop and driving through the pick-up window at Taco Bueno. No one assumed I was visiting royalty, or a pageant contestant. Everyone guessed it was my birthday. Maybe that was the point.

Maybe.

Or I might have been making up for the lost years when I didn't play princess as a little girl. Maybe it was because my youthful glow was fading and it was time to make friends with a different kind of beauty, one that requires collagen enhancement and space age facial primers. Perhaps I secretly wished I had been a beauty queen, starving myself into a Barbie-sized evening gown and spraying my jiggly bits with rubber cement for the bikini competition.

Then again, my desire to be crowned may not have been all frivolous fantasy and anorexia envy. Maybe I liked the tiara because I was finally comfortable enough in my own skin to wear something on the outside that matched how I felt on the inside—all princess and shimmer. Not to mention the power a tiara confers. Wonder Woman wears one. So does She-Ra. And Holly Golightly rocked a tiara in *Breakfast at Tiffany's*. Audrey Hepburn practically invented the cigarette holder, Empire State hair and the little black dress in that movie.

That princess fantasy might not be so bad after all. I can't go back in time or acquire super powers, but I can wear the tiara, its halo of rhinestone glory sparkling in an outward symbol of my inner magnificence.

My daughter was not born to be a patent and grosgrain girl, but the five bottles of sparkly nail polish on her nightstand give me some relief. Then I spotted the dresses.

Hanging in her closet, above the chaos of shin guards, journals, and half-finished friendship bracelets, were seven years worth of Easter frill. Fluffy and pristine in hues of soft lavender, buttery yellow, and peachy pink. Seven supremely feminine frocks complete with lace and chiffon, tulle and taffeta. I wrapped them carefully and transferred them to another closet, where they will stay until she has grown far beyond a girl. Collected, they show me I haven't entirely neglected my daughter's feminine foundation. She is not a girly-girl, but she has a set of dresses, tied up in a bow, that prove she was a princess—at least seven times. And she can be one again any time she wants. All she has to do is put on a tiara.

I might even let her borrow mine.

The Most Wonderful Time of the Year

CONTRARY TO THE SONG, Christmas is not the most wonderful time of the year. It is actually the darkest, most fattening, and interpersonally volatile time of the year. But that would make for terrible lyrics.

Every year I attempt to hide my pessimism (and my excessive vodka consumption) in favor of delivering a Grinch-less holiday experience for my children. Annually, I determine to create visions of sugarplums dancing inside their sleeping heads.

When they were little I decided to buy them each an ornament every year. I planned for a far away future when I'd hand them a box with twenty or so Christmas ornaments to remind them of home, family tradition, and their happy childhoods. Intermixed with the rest of our ornaments, my children now have motley collections of reindeer, Santas, and snowmen—each marked with their names and the date. They are eleven and thirteen now. Each year they search out their own trinkets and reminisce before setting them in places of honor upon the tree.

Aside from near toxic levels of dairy intake, this is our only holiday tradition. There are foods I might prepare this year or that; we spend the day at home or away; and Santa was long ago replaced by a kid in a blue Best Buy polo. I've even stopped dragging my family to church, but only because I feared the holy water might melt them like the Wicked Witch of the West. Last year I lured them to midnight services with the promise of carrying fire around a church. So naturally, that was the year the congregation elected to forgo the candle element of the candlelight service, which we might have known if church were a regular part of our week. Times like this I wonder if it should be.

Although our family has yet to—and truthfully may never—find our "church home," we are consumers of Christmas pageantry nonetheless. At least, that's what I thought. When my daughter was about six, she asked about a nativity scene; she wanted to know why Jesus was in that "hay thingy."

The hay thingy.

"The manger?"

My daughter smiled in her cherubic way, innocent and oblivious.

Surely, she knew that the Lord and Savior's bed was commonly referred to as a manger. The Christmas Eve story is one of the main stories, after all. For crying out loud, she played an angel in the Christmas pageant. That one time, when she was two. But still, who doesn't know manger? What kind of apple-pie eating American child living smack dab in the heartland doesn't know about the baby Jesus in the barn?

That was when I realized there are certain things your

children are not going to learn through osmosis or the culture at large. Even putting that cute nativity scene out on the dining room table is not enough. If you want them to know about mangers, you need to take them to church. However, that's tough for a family of occasional Christians... progressive Christians... Heathens, if you will, living in the Bible belt. We had tried several churches, but nothing really stuck. I even joined the neighborhood Bible study, where I might have fit in better if I hadn't thrown the word "metaphor" around like a brazen harlot.

The closest we've been to church lately was turning around in the parking lot of the gigantic gift shop-equipped house of worship with the million dollar crosses, man-made pond, and enormous banners that hang like billboards over its concrete walls to advertise the services offered for the current holiest day.

"See, Mom," my daughter said as I maneuvered through the beautifully landscaped parking lot. "We *do* go to church."

She's going to be a lawyer.

This Christmas we let the kids open most of their gifts on December 21st, before driving fourteen hours to a New Mexican ski resort for the season of cream-filled indulgence. On the way home, my daughter realized we hadn't opened ornaments. Somewhere between travel planning, un-fluffed artificial tree limbs, and the glass ball confetti that was once organized boxes of décor, I had neglected the only constant in our holiday season. But did they really want ornaments? These too-cool children, poised on the edge of being teenagers, all ear buds and eye rolls?

Yes, they assured me. The ornaments were a must. Shopping for them made the top of my post-vacation to-do list.

I spent a while with the clearance rack cast-offs before settling on two glass gingerbread people, matching but not identical. As we were technically into the New Year's portion of the year, I didn't bother to wrap them. Instead, I laid them on top of the piles I had made on the dining room table, my half-hearted attempt to sort out the holiday mess of mismatched garlands and broken angels.

My son asked about his ornament. "It's there," I said, nodding to the pile.

"I see it!" He picked up one of the gingerbread men. "Is this mine or Gaby's?"

He giggled when I showed him the other one—just like a little kid at Christmas. Then he took the ornaments upstairs to show his sister.

My children may never get the Bible stories quite right and our traditions may be sparse, but we take our joy where we find it. The most wonderful time of the year really does exist, so long as we remember it only lasts a moment.

As for the manger, we'll keep trying.

I hear the candles are back at midnight mass.

Red Light, Green Light, Shut the F^*k Up

THE ELEMENTARY SCHOOL MY CHILDREN attended is known in our town as the "private" public school. Located in the heart of gated and un-gated upper middle class neighborhoods, the percentage of children on free and reduced school lunches is zero and the biggest challenge some parents must overcome is Botox paralysis.

We affluent parents—real or perceived—are involved parents. We have certain expectations. We want our children to get the very best education money can buy, even at the free public school. Because we pay our taxes, damn it. Every child must have the best teacher, deserves to be in the gifted and talented program, and get a solo in the first grade production of *Are You There Winter, It's Me, Culturally Confused*.

We are, in short, a complete pain in the ass.

I like to think I'm different than the others. But I'm not. I'm just not interested in butting into the same things. This is not because I do not value education. I know my children will be more than okay with or without my parental intrusion at school. (It's elementary school, remember?) The teachers do not need my ill-informed micromanaging of rubrics and handouts. They don't need my expertise at bulletin board design. They could do without my passively aggressive concern about the child whose booger picking is disrupting my prodigy's crayon selection.

I like to think I'm all hands-off. And yet, there was that lunchroom issue.

Complaints about the school's unreasonable noise ordinance had been raging for months. Years maybe. But it all came to a crashing crescendo when I ate lunch with my fifth grade son one day. Eventually there would be a stoplight that turned from green to yellow, to red, whence there'd be Hell to pay. But this was before all that. This was during the time school administrators used a primitive cup system to keep kids quiet. A red cup was placed on the table, and if the children got too loud a monitor turned the cup upside down signaling that the kids were no longer allowed to talk.

At all.

What constituted too loud? Anything spoken above a low tone to the child directly next to them was deemed a noise infraction. Under no circumstances were these above average children allowed to speak to the person across the table. This type of insubordination was both unthinkable and punishable to the full extent of the principal's authority.

The day I came for lunch, my son and his friends were not talking at all. Their cup had been turned. "You were that noisy already?" I said. "You just got here."

The kids looked defeated. They did not speak. My son very quietly explained that the cup had been turned over the day before. They were on holdover punishment! I looked at the school creed painted on the wall, the one that pretentiously incorporated the word sagacious. (Tenacious wasn't enough, they needed to rhyme.) I tried to summon calm as I read the clause, "yesterday's mistakes are behind me," but calm wouldn't come. With the sass of a fifth-grader and the authority of a mother who had stood up to multiple pediatricians and the occasional politician, I turned the cup over. "Talk it up, kids. I'll take the heat."

I was, of course, an instant hero to the half dozen kids at the table. To the lunch monitors, I was the anti-Christ. The children and I enjoyed a lovely lunch full of low decibel laughter and conversation. The lunch monitors and I exchanged icy glances, but before they had a chance to tell on me, I went to see the principal. She was less than reasonable. You would be too if your office was located right across the hall from the cafeteria full of children. Those kids file in there every single day and proceed to make a serious racket. But isn't that what human beings do? Isn't it right and normal and important to socialize while having a meal? Isn't breaking bread together, in fact, a much more important skill than coloring the continents or diagramming sentences?

The principal did not see it that way. When I told her that if she walked into any restaurant during the lunch hour she would hear the same chaotic and joyful din, she said that kind of behavior had no place in school. She went on and on about the noise. And I get it, I do. I can't stand being around a bunch of kids either. The sound of them would drive me to keep bourbon in my World's Greatest Teacher mug. And I don't even drink brown liquor. Which is why I'm not a teacher. Or a principal. It is also the reason I have doors that lock on my home office.

"I don't think you have a noise problem," I told her. "I think you have an architectural problem."

Surely they could send those kids to eat lunch in the gym, way down the hall from the principal's office. Wouldn't that solve everything?

No. No, it would not, I was told.

In fact, the cups weren't working either. Seems the fear factor of lunch lady glares was fading. School is no place for energetic children, and these particular students were getting out of control. Something had to be done before a full-scale revolt ensued. What they really needed was a civil engineering solution.

I can only imagine the principal's glee when the stoplight was installed. The children took their cues by watching its tones of red, yellow and green, while the lunch ladies were free to police illegal snack trading. Under the watchful eye of the stoplight, the kids tried not to chew too loudly. They dreamed of the day they could talk about recess with the boy across the table.

Fortunately, the stoplight did not last long. I don't know what let to its removal, because, like I said, I try to stay out of school politics. But I suspect some of those pain-in-the-ass parents got together and visited the principal. For that,

I'm grateful, but I just hope they don't expect any of their kids to land the lead in the winter program. My child was born to play the Snowman King.

Olympic Glory, Again?

THE FIVE-CIRCLED EMBLEM IN THE LOWER left corner of my television screen reminds me. The Olympics are coming. Again.

Seriously?

The Summer ones?

Again?

I'm not really into the Olympics. Never been good at sports. Never understood the appeal of watching people who are. However, after watching any gymnastics competition, I entertained the neighbors by pretending to be Nadia Comaneci on the imaginary balance beam in the front yard. But my fantasy Olympic striving, discipline, and sheer love of sport never lasted long. My body was not built for athletics, and my psyche not suited to epic rivalry.

Olympic competition doesn't excite me, but the camaraderie does. I enjoy the games vicariously through those that root for underdogs and cheer for gold and silver, preferably near an open bag of Doritos and a Diet Coke. I like to sit next to my husband while he critiques a high diver's form and explains the rules of soccer. Again. Because in a hundred years I will still not be clear on the "off sides" of futbol. During this Olympics I will be watching the passage of time, mine and my children's. I am captivated by the bookmarking effect of this communal event and its ability to place time in context.

Parental time is complicated. It's split. There is the small part that passes in our own lives, and then there is the significant part that passes in our children's lives. This occurs simultaneously, the same period of time that is collapsed in our own lives is expanded in our children's.

Although it feels like yesterday to me, four years have passed since we celebrated hot weather athletics, determination, and seriously cut abs. When I was a child the interval between Olympics seemed a lifetime. Four years. That was the difference between eating paste and writing book reports. It was the difference between changing gears on a ten-speed and changing gears in your first stick shift. I can only imagine my own children are experiencing four years the way I did— as an eternity. And now, as we watch together, I see these past four years as the difference between their childhood and their coming young adulthood.

The last time we watched the summer Olympics, my children were eight and ten. Every sport was new and exciting, or at least an excuse to stay up late. This summer is one of our last chances to see the steeplechasers, the gymnasts, and the incessant news coverage with our children while they are still children. It's an excuse to come together. This year we will watch with purpose. Track: because my son runs. Soccer: because my daughter plays. My husband and children will get caught up in the competition and glory of it all, while I will notice how Ocean Spray and Metamucil work the Olympics into their marketing.

With a hormone-fueled enthusiasm, my son will join my husband watching beach volleyball. And then in August I will explain to my daughter why she can't wear short-shorts to school. We will watch stories about the oldest and youngest Olympians, and take in the sights of London, captured beautifully in HD at all the right angles. Who knows, I may even catch a renewed enthusiasm to "pick up running" again.

When we come together to watch the Olympics this year, I hope time passes slowly. (I'll deal with the Doritos fallout come September.) In another blink it will be time for the summer Olympics again. And next time my son will packing for college.

They Don't Call Me Mommy Anymore

Of Scissors and Scotch Tape

I GOT UP AT FOUR IN THE MORNING. Crazy, I know, but my husband does it one day every week so sometimes I show my solidarity by getting up with him. It's a bad idea, a pointless show of support that usually does not end well, but if I'm lucky I get a lot of work done before the kids wake up. On this particular morning I paid bills, cleared my inbox, and worked out a four-leg carpool schedule for my children's cotillion class. We can all rest assured the children will be on time to the classes where they learn to say hello and where-do-you-go-to-school to a member of the opposite sex without shaking, sweating, or humping a leg.

One of my morning desk jobs required tape. It was urgent, in the way that only Scotch tape emergencies can be. But I'm nothing if not prepared and I took comfort in the knowledge that my trusty tape would be there, waiting patiently in my top left desk drawer.

Wrong.

My heart raced as the swell of anger grew. Such a mildly

sticky substance should never cause this much distress. However, instances of lost tape have become a peeve of mine, along with missing scissors and borrowed mechanical pencils. I need little to practice my trade and manage the myriad amusements of our family. All I ask is that my simple tools remain in, or are returned to their proper homes. Is that so much to ask?

My children are infatuated with tape. They make things out of it—pictures, shoes, bicycle parts. They write notes on tape, and then tape them onto walls with more tape. They stick it to their faces. They make out with it. They're totally going to have a double wedding with Scotch and masking. Duct will be the Maid of Honor.

Me? I just use tape. And when my little stick buddy isn't where I left it, I get pissy.

I looked in the drawer, in the office supply cubby, and behind the bookshelf. No tape. At least three rolls of it—gone, vanished without a trace, like tissue in cold season. Maybe it was the hour, or my not quite fully caffeinated state, but I was livid. I wanted that tape. I wanted it NOW. But it was five-thirty in the morning. Instead of rousing my children from their beds in a mad woman's frenzy, I plotted revenge. I would teach those ingrates the consequences of stealing a woman's tape. It's not like they hadn't been warned. A few weeks earlier, I'd stocked up. And not just for me. Generously, I provided each of my two children with a personal roll of tape.

"This is yours," I said. "You can let me know if you need more, but under no circumstances are you to take the tape from my drawer." I had showed them the two rolls of tape in my desk drawer so as to underscore the importance of this directive.

"Got it?"

After the expected number of eye rolls, they answered in unison. "Yes, Mom, we got it."

Clearly, they didn't get it.

Before finishing my pre-dawn cup of coffee I devised a surprisingly rational plan. I would simply take the cost of the replacement office supplies out of their allowances. Each time I reached for something of mine that was not where it should be—cha-ching, show me your money.

When my son and daughter came down for breakfast I said good morning, hugged them, and calmly announced the new policy. One set of eyes narrowed, then teared up. The other just rolled back in its annoyed 'tween skull.

Voices were raised.

The toaster was abused.

Corn flake shrapnel flew.

My daughter was most visibly upset, as she values money more than her brother does, more than shoes, more than breath, I sometimes fear. She shook while pleading her case of injustice.

"You just want to make money off us!"

Ah... yes, exactly. Exploitation of my children popped into my head shortly after peeing on the stick. My wicked plan to get rich extorting my own money for Scotch tape and paperclips was finally starting to pay off! And boy, was I in for a windfall with the scissors.

I resumed typical morning activities—cooking for my children, cleaning up after my children, writing checks so that my children can read books and attend enriching extra-curricular activities. However, I soon noticed that neither of them were speaking to me. Perhaps I'd been a bit harsh, a bit reactive. It occurred to me that picking a fight about tape over breakfast might not have been the wisest choice. And yes, I wondered if it was actually my husband who had taken the tape. But I had to stand my ground. This is the new normal, tape thieves. Deal with it. Because once you go too far down a road you need to stay the course or accept a kind of parental defeat that undermines every future disciplinary effort.

God help us if someone ever swipes the three-hole punch.

Promises To My Teenagers

I RECENTLY SPENT TIME AROUND a table with some older and wiser mothers. Conversation soon turned to teenagers. And there I was, sitting with the grownups. I envied my own budding members of the maligned demographic, who sat on the hostess's matching recliners, lost in competition on their iPods, while the battle-worn women told of children morphing into angry, emotionally unstable, abusive—even suicidal—teens.

"You never want to believe it will happen to you," said one. "You never want to believe that your sweet child will change."

I smiled and nodded and kept quiet, because here's the thing: I don't believe it. Call me naïve, call me smug, call me a delusional Pollyanna, but I do not believe my children will ever become the dreadful creatures described around that table. I'm clueless, I know. It's the only way to be an optimist. And I hold to my conviction even in the face of empirical evidence to the contrary. My son is often apathetic and entitled, rude and vulgar. Still, I'm in denial. I don't believe my kids will become unpleasant in the same way that I don't believe the economic sky is falling or that I'll die from drinking aspartame. Besides, teenagers have a right to be surly. What if some middle-aged couple controlled your life?

I needed a plan, a code to live by, insurance against the maternal negativity. Kids, this one's for you. I might not be a cool mom, I don't want to be your friend, but I pledge to believe in your innate awesomeness and support your unique charm. At least, I'll do my best. Here's what you can count on:

I promise to buy as much acne medication as I can afford.
My dear children, you have inherited not only your father's enviable olive skin tone, but also his overzealous sebaceous glands. Your grandparents, who place Advil and Oxycontin in the same pharmaceutical category, did not believe in acne intervention and your father seems predisposed to this viewpoint. Not to worry. I will keep you in benzoyl peroxide, exfoliating crystals, and clarifying toner for as long as you need it.

I promise not talk to your friends on Facebook.
Don't get me wrong. I'll lurk, I'll snoop, I'll scrutinize and make decisions about your social life based on information I glean from your online networks (not to mention your text messages), but I will not engage your friends. I won't comment on your status, poke your hotter peers, or tag you in pictures with your grandmother. (You'll have to deal with her directly about her policy.)

LELA DAVIDSON

I promise to let you have ugly hair.

In *Peggy Sue Got Married*, Nicholas Cage's character Charlie says, "What's the point of being a teenager if you can't dress weird?" Same goes for hair. So go ahead, gorgeous daughter, get a Mohawk. See if I care. It'll grow. Ratty t-shirts? Ridiculous makeup? Go for it. I draw the line at tattoos and facial piercing. Only after you've proven your skill at long-term planning by sticking with a course of study long enough to earn a degree will you earn the right to make permanent decisions about body decor.

I promise to accept that you will have sex.

Eventually. But please, for the love of latex, do not let me catch you doing it. I realize that your sex-education so far has consisted of abstinence-only propaganda and STD fear mongering. You know I don't not expect or recommend you wait until marriage to have sex. But if you could please just hold off until you go [away] to college, I will show my appreciation with a crate of condoms.

I promise to pay for college.

Speaking of school, it's on me. I may never let you forget the luxury you enjoy, but as long as I'm breathing and you're studying, you'll never have to wonder if you can afford an education. Get good grades and don't end up in an episode of Frat Boys Gone Wild, and I'll pick up the tab. (If you really love me, you'll stay off Greek Row entirely.)

I don't ask much in return for all this. Just don't be a jerk. And don't turn me into one of those women sitting around a table in fifteen years lamenting, "You never want to believe it will happen to you."

My Daughter, the Stylist

My DAUGHTER ASKED ME TO GO SHOPPING yesterday—clothes shopping. This was a first. Until now, we've shopped for her or we've shopped for me, but we haven't "gone shopping" together. I was excited to get her buy-in on her own wardrobe, but I had ulterior motives, too. My daughter, you see, is also my personal stylist.

"Mom, can we shop somewhere else this time? Besides *Old Navy*?"

But... I have coupons, and reward points, and—

"Like, can we go to *Aeropostale*? And *Forever21*?"

While Gaby is particular about what she wears, her tomboy chic has not yet required daylong excursions. Her uniform has been easy: Jeans—the rattier the better—a camisole tank with a t-shirt over top, bunched up in a ponytail holder in the back. That's it. Every day.

Every.

Day.

Not exactly chic, but it's clean and covered up. I can't

complain. I've always wished, however, that she were a tiny bit more girly. It might have been my fault for swaddling her in broken-in dinosaur receiving blankets. Maybe when I dressed her in big brother's hand-me-downs football onesies I should have foreseen future ice rinks, where she would play hockey instead of carve circles while wearing chiffon and sequins. I tried to make up for my mistake during the preschool years, but it was too late. I dressed her up in seersucker dresses and matching bloomers for a couple of years, but by PreK she took a stand, quickly adopting a pants-only policy. I tried to frill up her closet with bright corduroys and matchy sweaters, but it didn't work. No Davidson will ever forget the Easter standoff of 2007. Lime green and I lost big that day. The battle put an end to my foolishness forever and firmly established who controlled what Gaby wore.

Since then it's been strictly jeans and t-shirts. Until now. Oh, the possibilities! I wanted to make a day of it, go to lunch and get a pedicure, but I had to play it cool. I would NOT skip from store to store singing like a deranged Julie Andrews who just found new curtains to slice up.

We found an adorable top at Charlotte Russe. "That is SO cute," my daughter said.

"You're right, that is super cute."

"It would look SO good on you. Can we share it?"

Share a shirt? Things were moving quickly, indeed. Fortunately, back in the dressing room we discovered the top didn't look right on either one of us. We did, however, find the perfect jeans—for her—and because they were buy one get one half off, I searched for a pair for myself. Since I am past my prime for skinny cut skinnies, I searched for a nice boot cut—the new Mom Jeans. They didn't have those, so I tried something with industrial grade Spandex. The sales girl only snickered once, but the only opinion that mattered was my girl's.

"They make your legs look demented." She's direct. We left with two identical pair of jeans for her, and a couple of age-appropriate tops for me.

I have no idea where my anti-fashion daughter gets her style instincts, but they are always right. Since first grade she has held veto power over my outfits. Anytime I come home with something I'm not quite sure about, she confirms my suspicions and back to *TJ Maxx* it goes. My clothing lives and dies by her judgments. It's like having Stacy London on speed dial, except I can just yell up the stairs. Or, better yet, now—take her into the dressing room. As long as I continue to pass Gaby's inspection I'll never be one of those 40-some-things who think it's okay to shop at *Justice* so long as they can squeeze into a junior size fourteen. Color me Forever-Grateful.

I realize I'm working in a very small window of opportunity, a brief moment in time that my daughter will want to go to the mall with me. Soon her interest in shopping with me will begin and end with my Mastercard. But this time was bliss. She even remembered to thank me when we got home. And I only have to return one tiny little dress to *Forever21*—the one she told me not to buy.

Show Me the Real Texts

THIS MORNING I ASKED MY SON about a friend of his, who happens to be a girl. In response, he sighed and rolled his eyes.

"So you're not going to tell me anything?" I asked. "Ever?"

No response.

"I tell *you* stuff."

He looked me in the eye. "Okay, let me read your text messages."

"You want to read my text messages?"

"Yes."

"You want to read MY text messages?"

"Uh-huh."

"YOU want to read my text messages?"

"See. Told you."

I took out my phone and began reading a scintillating conversation I'd had (in full sentences) with a girlfriend. Perhaps he sensed that I did not read the part where we switched from professional pursuits to her out-of-town date. Maybe he intuitively knew I'd left out my advice to "Wear sexy underwear."

"Show me the REAL text messages."

Challenge accepted. Following are my incoming messages, in no particular order, on any particular day:

- Can you give me directions to your house?
- Thank you for following me [less exciting than it sounds]
- I have a weakness for petit fours
- Make sure you bring your email receipt to prove you paid
- Any hotties at the Chamber? [of Commerce]
- Thanks for the helpful advice, as always [sarcastic]
- Mr. Snowman has found his purpose in life [not sarcastic]
- Tell me again why I'm wearing a toga?
- Down girl
- Is your projector Mac compatible?
- Cash, fool!
- Please don't check me in on Facebook
- I'm good, need to pee
- No Spanx? That is awesome!
- One of the ladies to my left is talking about passing stones

See? Innocuous, every last one. Out of context. So long as he never finds my secret decoder ring, we're good.

Hooters at the Hockey Game

FOR FOUR YEARS MY DAUGHTER played ice hockey. She was the only girl on her team. We'd travel to other cities and see ponytails hanging out of two, three, even four helmets. Girls played alongside the boys all over the Midwest, but not on our team. Gaby was the only girl hockey player in all of Northwest Arkansas. She loved the attention, and providing rock solid defense. And she did it in pink. We searched pro shops at every ice rink from Illinois to Texas for helmets, jerseys, stick tape—anything pink. Coaches, parents and players all cheered for our star: "Gaby rocks in pink socks!"

Hockey in the Midwest means traveling, and we usually traveled as a family, but with two on the ice, schedules occasionally conflict. One weekend my daughter and I drove to St. Louis while my husband and son headed south to Dallas for another tournament. Several families took separate highways that weekend, and the dads on a kitchen pass took a wrong turn the first night—to *Hooters*. My daughter and I heard about it the next morning when one of the un-chaperoned fathers gushed over dry powdered eggs and a greasy bacon facsimile.

"They took pictures with the boys and everything!"

With the big boys, too? I wondered. Wow, generous. How many times had they swiped their credit cards for that honor? Gaby and I ate defrosted pancakes while this man who should have been a role model relayed tales of shorts and wings. His son did not speak.

"See you at the rink," I said. "I have to go explain to my ten-year-old what a *Hooters* girl is."

The ride to the rink wasn't nearly long enough for that conversation.

The locker room buzzed. Apparently the *Hooters* girls had told the boys they'd to come to the game.

"You wish," said one of the moms.

It might have been me.

But the dads were sure the girls would show up to cheer for the boys. One could only hope they'd cheer for my girl, too. Maybe they'd bring her a uniform so her teammates could shout, "Gaby scores in orange shorts!"

One little boy told me he'd met the girl he was going to marry.

"Aim high," I told him. Then I felt bad. There's not a damn thing wrong with earning your way by hustling tips in suntan pantyhose. It wasn't the girls I had a problem with.

I got my daughter into her pink socks and onto the ice while a few dads tried to hush their sons. Under my silent but deadly maternal gaze, some of them were properly embarrassed. Or maybe what I sensed was fear. Their wives' phone numbers were programmed into my phone and I'd recently learned how to group text. The few men who failed to see the error of their ways continued to glow at the prospect of breasts in sweaters. I got Gaby dressed and taped her stick, repressing my urge to go on a Nicholson rampage a la *The Shining*—but only because it would have broken the stick.

With my girl suited and ready, I made my way to the stands, where moms buzzed with talk of *Hooters* girls and other women's unfortunate choices of husbands. We mocked the idiot men who naively believed their waitresses would show. Nobody tips that good.

You can imagine our surprise when two silken-haired coeds strolled toward us. Hooter Dad hopped around the bleachers to usher the girls to their places of honor. They watched, we won, more gushing ensued, and many eyes rolled. And then we ate Sonic.

But wait, there's more.

The following Monday I received an email from Hooter Dad. He was beyond excited because the manager of his new favorite *Hooters* had contacted him about a story they were submitting to the national *Hooters* magazine. Awesome! Maybe my kid would make the centerfold. I read down the email to Hooter Dad's original message to the restaurant's manager. It went something like this:

"On behalf of the Northwest Arkansas Youth Hockey League, I want to thank your entire staff, especially Candie and Stormie, for the amazing service and extra attention paid to our boys! These girls are SUCH professionals. They blew all our minds with their EXTREME generosity!"

LELA DAVIDSON

And yes, I made up those names to protect the innocent. This man certainly did not speak for me, so on behalf of myself, I took several cleansing breaths before responding. Fully oxygenated, fingers perched over the keyboard, I was preparing to let him have it when an email from the coach landed in my inbox. He kindly requested that Hooter Dad refrain from representing anything "on behalf of" our league. There was a tone.

None of it would have been necessary if they'd just gone to Applebee's.

Other moms called me. How was Gaby doing? Would she be scarred for life? Was I livid? To which I answered: Fine, no, and not anymore. Irritated as I was that my little girl had to hear grown men sigh over girls only a few years older than herself, and watch her teammates lose their focus over female anatomy, at least she got to see first hand what goes on in a locker room. You can't blame the boys; they're under the influence of their fathers. You can't blame the dads; they're under the spell of the girls. And you certainly can't blame the girls for being young, beautiful, and apparently interested in youth hockey.

But that Hooter Dad—him I'd like to batter and fry and serve to an all-women's hockey team. Instead I'll have to take comfort in believing that, like a bucket full of chicken wings, he's all skin and no meat.

How Not to Get STDs

THE WELL-CHILD PHYSICALS WERE ONLY a formality, an annual exercise to make sure the kids didn't have scoliosis or rickets. We make the pilgrimage primarily to get release forms signed. Shooting the kids full of state-mandated vaccinations is a bonus. Schedule-wise, it was a two-parents-required afternoon, and my son and I had beaten my husband and daughter to the doctor's office. While we waited, the nurse reviewed the immunization records. My 13-year-old son was due for a meningitis vaccine. My 11-year-old daughter needed that, as well as a diptheria/pertussis/tetanus booster, in case she steps on a rusty nail in a third world country—or the Arkansas delta.

"They can both get the Gardasil shot, too," the nurse told me. "It's optional, but it's a good idea."

I had no problems with the HPV inoculation. What's one more shot, right? And one that prevents genital warts and dysplasia? Sign us up! But it's all about timing. Gardasil is given in three doses over a period of six months. And you have to catch the children before they come in contact with the virus. In other words, before they start having sex. That's why they start so young—eleven in my daughter's case. Because she was due for two vaccinations already—the kind that prevent diseases you can get from sickly transients and possibly my own dishwasher on a bad day—I decided to hold off on the STD insurance for both of my children.

"We've got time," I told the nurse. I turned to my son. "You're not sexually active yet, are you?" He gave me a wide-eyed head shake.

The nurse smiled, then lowered her voice almost to a whisper, "But he can get it from toilet seats."

Excuse me?

Did this presumably licensed medical professional just imply—no *say*—that my son could contract the HPV virus from a toilet seat? I tried to give her the benefit of the doubt, tried to assume she was pushing Gardasil purely for profit and not because she actually believed my child could contract a venereal disease from an inanimate porcelain object. (Then again, who knows how this woman interacts with her plumbing.) I didn't know how to respond, so I addressed my son instead.

"Just so you know, if you come home with genital warts, I'm not buying any toilet seat excuse."

As I sat there waiting for the valedictorian of her nursing class to return, I imagined how mortifying it would have been to have the Gardasil conversation with my own mother at thirteen, much less eleven. Call me old-fashioned, but this was the pediatrician's office. It's tough to reconcile talk of STDs with the *Dora the Explorer* books in the rack. In my day we handled sex the old fashioned way; we learned from someone's older sister how to get condoms and birth control pills at *Planned Parenthood*. And we waited until high school.

Both of my children are much too young for sex, but I realize that when the time comes, it'll be like flipping a switch. No warning, no build up, just sex. So far, my son still confides in me. He sought my advice when he was planning to kiss a girl for the first time. I told him to ask her first. Also, that he might not be ready. Beyond that, he'd have to consult his dad for logistics. I was relieved when he told me it didn't work out. Because it's a quick jaunt from kissing to genital warts. Not to mention grandchildren.

After the nurse had been gone a few minutes—presumably entering incorrect information into my son's medical records—she poked her head back into the room. Again, she addressed me, not my son.

"I checked with the doctor," she said. "It's 'mucous membrane to mucous membrane.' That's how you get it," she said.

Which was exactly what they told us all those years ago at *Planned Parenthood*. Beware the mucous membranes. They get you into trouble every time. At least I didn't have to hear it sitting next to my mother in front of a jungle mural.

Frickin' Is Not an Adjective

WE WERE AT THE DINNER TABLE THE other day, tortur-
ing my son before letting him open his birthday present. We
had caved to his request for *Call of Duty Black Ops*, because
we are awesome parents who donated their standards to
Goodwill with the Diaper Genie and the Tickle Me Elmo. My
just-turned-thirteen-year-old knew what his gift was, but I
wanted to prolong his anticipation.

"We got you *Dora the Explorer*," I said, passing the pasta.

"No, you didn't."

"Yes, we did."

"Whatever."

"Would you like that?" I asked. "If we bought you Dora?
Or would you be SO mad?"

He was quick to answer. Too quick. Just as the noodles
hit his plate, his answer escaped, "No, I'd f*ckin' love it."

Time stopped for just an instant. I think that's what
some would call a defining moment. My reality was irrevo-
cably altered. My little boy just said the forbidden word, the

Big Kahuna, the F-Bomb. Right there over grilled chicken and zucchini. And naturally, he laughed like an idiot.

I showed more self-control.

I looked at my husband who appeared not to have noticed, then back to my son. "You can't say that."

John suddenly made the connection. "Did he just say—?" He looked at Zander. "Did you?"

"I didn't say it!" He shook his head. "Seriously."

"Yes, you did."

"No, I said frickin'."

"No, you didn't," I told him. "I heard you."

"Well, you heard wrong."

What's worse than profanity at the dinner table? Talking back to your mother in a way that implies she is old.

My husband summoned the closest threat. "I will pull you out of that school!"

Really, Dear? The school we put him in? The school he didn't really want to go to in the first place? The one where they make him wear the uniforms and don't let boys and girls eat lunch together? If this was as good as my husband could offer, clearly it was up to me to bring pain upon this child.

I had nothing.

Frickin' is not an adjective. And yet, it is—perfectly acceptably in mainstream media and the mouths of those unwilling to embrace it's grittier ancestor. I don't like it on principle. If you're going to swear, just do it. Call me a purist. Still, I'm not ready to hear either f-word from my kids. Maybe I never will be. Hearing my son talk like that for the first time left me conflicted. What he'd said was funny, and I admired the quick delivery. But, of course I couldn't admit that. Or could I? The next day a friend told me how she'd had to bite her tongue so she wouldn't laugh when her ten-year-old son tearfully admitted to calling the school yard bully a motherf*cker.

When do we get to give up the mature Mommy façade? And where is the line between being honest with our kids and raising vulgar smartasses? Maybe that night at dinner I should have shocked him right back with a hearty, "F*ck, yeah. That's the spirit!"

Or not.

Better to blame it on video games and pour a second glass of wine.

Date Night, Family Style

MY HUSBAND IS A FAMILY MAN. Big time. So for his recent birthday I took us all on a surprise family date. I didn't
tell anyone where we were going, only that they had to wear
something clean and relatively free of holes and frayed edges.
A block from the restaurant I told them we were headed to
Ruth's Chris.

"We just won't pay the mortgage this month," I said.

My husband did a little victory fist-yes—for the meal
ahead, not the damage to our credit score. The kids just
looked at each other. They didn't get my joke until they
opened the menu.

"Eighty-three bucks for a steak?" my son said. "Who's
paying for this?" He knows I won't even buy brand name ce-
real. "Because I want to eat for the rest of the week, too."

After pointing out that the eighty-three dollar steak was
for two, we moved on to the appetizer portion of the evening.
My husband told the kids not to "fill up on bread." Some
version of this is spoken at every dinner we eat away from

home. At the pizza place he says, "Don't fill up on crackers." At the Mexican place it's, "Don't fill up on chips." And at the sushi joint, "Stop gorging yourselves on edamame!" Never mind that no child of mine has ever passed up a slice of pepperoni pizza or a chimichanga because they were too full of pre-meal carbs. If they balk at eating raw fish, I hesitate to blame a soybean.

The ambiance was ideal for any date night, family or otherwise. It was dark, cozy, and candlelit. Metallic stars sparkled on the tablecloth, just like the ones on the night I met my husband in 1991. Instead of littering a sticky bar table, these were scattered atop crisp white cotton. Still, they brought back a flood of memories and a feeling of awe at how far we've come together—my husband and me—at the family we had created, now gathered around this finely laid table, complete with a solicitous waitress who tidied up after our over-indulgence in bread with the most impressive technology my mildly OCD son had ever encountered: the crumb blade.

"You need to get one of these at home, Mom."

Never mind that we are not crumb people, but rather gloppy mess of cheese dip people.

After removing our crumbs, the waitress spent a long time explaining how the steaks would be prepared in 1,800-degree ovens. There was much discussion about the "very hot plates" much like there is at the Mexican place. My daughter was skeptical that the plates would really be 1,800 degrees. Luckily, when the steaks came out, she was too busy with her knife and fork to test her theory. Her eyes got huge with the first bite, as she is our little Carnivorous Fabulous.

"This steak is amazing!" she said after swallowing a cave-girl-sized bite. Oh, the manners. She might have learned to pick up a T-bone and gnaw off the flesh at home, but we hoped they had beaten that out of her at cotillion.

Season One tuition: $150.

Dresses, gloves, hose, and after parties: $362.

Raising a girl who will never be a cheap date: priceless.

As if the children and the wine and incredible meat weren't enough, we entertained ourselves guessing the ages of a couple across the room. They looked like a coach and his star soccer player and sat much too close together on the same side of a booth. My son decided to get a closer look on the way to the bathroom. Or maybe I suggested that. Always training my children, always training. We were all eager to hear the report, but upon his return my son was excited about something else.

"Okay, first of all...the bathrooms? Amazing!" Yes, you read that right. The steak *and* the bathrooms, both amazing.

This moment is worth all the years of not taking my children to expensive restaurants regularly, not splurging on luxury vacations, not belonging to a country club. So that my 13-year-old son could be this impressed by a men's room. He then went on to assure us that the girl half of the couple at the booth in question was WAY younger than that old dude. It was appropriate that this bit of life knowledge was passed along family style, around the table with those who love each other most.

We laughed and ate. We made crumbs just to watch them

be whisked away. And sometime after the steaks and the bottle of Shiraz, John and I told the kids how we met—sticky table, tacky stars and all. And that was the most amazing part.

His Taste in Music

I HEARD THE MUSIC WHEN I PULLED into the garage. Vaguely familiar, oddly haunting, incredibly annoying. In the kitchen I found my daughter peacefully frosting cupcakes while overdramatic orchestral sounds blasted through my living room. And my daughter, singing along, "Sail away. Sail away. Sail away."

Enya.

How could this have happened? I had safeguarded against this moment, starting with a steady supply of AC/DC while she was in-utero and following up with all manner of classic rock, and other good music.

"Why are you listening to this?" I screamed over the inane lyrics.

She smiled and wiped chocolate off the edge of a cupcake before carefully placing it on a plate. "What?"

I set down my purse and looked for the remote control so I could turn down the volume.

"Did Daddy put this music on?"

My husband appeared in the hall, moving his head in time with the music. My daughter smiled again, watching him. They head bobbed at each other like the speakers were blaring *Motley Crue*.

Seems my daughter's reading teacher had been playing *Enya* during silent reading time. In my opinion *Enya* is not an improvement on silence. However, my daughter has been brainwashed. When she had mentioned her fondness for the one-named Celtic wonder to her father, he foraged like a lovesick leprechaun through the old collection of CDs. You remember those—flat shiny things that came wrapped in an infuriating plastic? Our collection of antiquated music on antiquated technology usually stays hidden in the closet under the stairs. For years the *Gypsy Kings*, *Salt-n-Pepa*, and *Enya* have been quietly slept behind the wrapping paper and the sewing machine.

Until now.

We can see traits already that will be passed down from John or myself to one or the other of our children. Zander is brilliant but sometimes too literal. He gets that from me. Gaby bottles her feelings up inside. Clearly Daddy's girl there. Zander has his father's engineering mind. Gaby is athletic. (We have no idea where that comes from.) But this musical taste. You always expect your kids to reach a certain age and embrace terrible music. Zander likes dubstep. But even that is better than the elevator music my husband likes. Smooth jazz, *Kenny G.*, that *Impanema* song. The sound of *Enya* brought back memories of every time I wanted to gouge my ears with a rusty Q-Tip.

My husband was so thrilled that our daughter had discovered his music, he did not stop with at one sample of mind-numbing nostalgia. He took this dangerous game further. As if *Enya* were not repetitive enough, he took their listening pleasure to the next level. I had forgotten (or blocked from memory) my husband's affinity for creepy techno music. *Enigma* brought it all back.

And it hurt.

Watching them enjoy the music together, I knew my protests were futile. There were genetics in play. But bad musical taste genes will not stop me from raging against the machine of ethereal synthesized un-music crap. I have to believe that someday she will rock hard, or at least choose music that has a good beat you can dance to. I have to believe there is hope.

Because if not, we have much to fear—like *Yaani*.

Test Flight

MY SON WENT TO CAMP THIS SUMMER. Not the kind with Jesus and archery. He visited the University of Kansas campus for a three-week fling with aerospace engineering. Because he scores well on standardized tests, Zander is invited to many Very Special Opportunities. The marketing for these academic enrichment programs consists of thinly veiled accusations that good parents prove their love and support by sending gifted children to tours of Greek ruins and space camps—in actual space.

Zander will be in eighth grade this year, which in the language of college entrance calendars, loosely translates to you'd-better-hurry-up-and-choose-a-major-or-risk-an-aimless-adulthood. Kids are supposed to start thinking about what they want to do in life in middle school, planning where they might want to study and building their resumes. At that age I was still collecting stickers and trying to figure out if culottes were friend or foe.

Society's expectations of 13-year-olds have changed.

That's why, when we received the glossy brochure for engineering camp, we didn't hesitate. Zander's SAT scores were so high that we could legally send him to college now. (The kid makes a mean ramen. He'd be fine.) Not only was he eligible for the camp, but his math score qualified him for the demanding engineering curriculum. Plus, the camp was run by Duke University. When a leading university sends you a text-merged-facsimile-signed letter, requesting your first-born to attend their elite summer science institute, you write a check. Maybe you then call some grandparents or sell a sibling to cover that check, but not until it's in the mail.

I didn't think we'd have to convince Zander that he wanted to go to camp. What teenage boy wouldn't want to spend the summer learning about lift, thrust, and—well, whatever else goes into flying stuff? But my son wasn't thrilled about spending his vacation doing math. He also admitted reluctance to being away from home for three weeks. Home is, after all, where the Xbox is. And the family. Zander is social, but not as interested in spending time with friends as family. Though he wasn't saying so, I knew he'd miss my stir-fried broccoli, the baby names I call him when I tuck him in at night, and his father's daily table manners assessment.

After weeks of pleas to his higher intelligence, it was food that finally closed the deal. I played the all-you-can-eat buffet card. This might have been a slight exaggeration, but that's how I interpret the word cafeteria. All you can eat. He'd thank me later. Once Zander was in, I had to work on my husband, who was devastated to learn from the camp

LELA DAVIDSON

handbook that parents were strongly discouraged from visiting on weekends. John had intended to drive the three and a half hours to—what?—tell our son to take his elbows off the table?

"He'll be fine," he said, to himself.

It took Zander less than five minutes to settle into the dorm room he'd be sharing with a kid from Houston. He joined a game of cards in the hall while we headed to the parent orientation, where the first order of business was homesickness. A young man who could have been a *Lord of the Rings* extra introduced himself as the counselor. He would work closely with children suffering from anxiety about being away from home. They had staff for that. I tried not to think about the tuition, but I was a bit anxious that Dr. Hobbit would probably earn more this summer than I would.

Next up: the teachers. They lined up against the wall and introduced themselves and their subjects. We waited while the vibrant young grad students and new professors provided their bios and their subjects: creative writing, medical science, English literature. The introductions progressed down the line, each one bringing us one closer to the paunchy guy with the white crew cut.

"I knew that was him," John told me later. "That is one old school hard-ass engineer." I wondered if Zander would ever forgive us for making him waste three precious *Halo* skill-building weeks on math camp with grandpa and his pocket protector.

But it was too late to back out now. The check had cleared, and once we had set up the new lamp and filled my son's nightstand with Ritz Bitz and Oreos, it was time to leave. The walk down the hall was short, the elevator ride painful, and the drive home too quiet. In the weeks that followed, John fared as expected.

"Did he call today?"

I felt sorry for him, and a little guilty. I was enjoying the relative break of managing only one child. Still, it wasn't all easy. I found myself taking my daughter to places she didn't belong because I didn't want to leave her home alone. But a girl's got to learn about Happy Hour some time. After a week, John sent Zander a care package, and started making plans to make the trip for the second to last day of camp, when Zander's class would perform a test flight of the gliders they engineered in class.

"Are other parents going to do that?"

My husband didn't answer. "Did he text?"

"Should he?"

"I thought maybe he would tell us about the dance."

Ah, yes, the dance. In addition to studying the principles that cause airplanes to stay in the air, the Boy and Girl Geniuses participated in many social events, such as movie night, scavenger hunts, and dances. Unlike actual college, there were no red Solo cups filled with assorted liquors. (Not that we know of.) We didn't get many details. Apparently describing awkward moments with the opposite sex is not the highlight of every 13-year-old's day. All we got were simple answers, delivered on cue. We had asked Zander to call at least once a day. And every night he did, right before he went to bed, and not because he wanted to hear our voices as a stand-in to being tucked in. He had a more practical reason to call us as late as possible, after he'd been checked into his room.

"I didn't want to waste any of my free time," he said.

I'm guessing he never visited the Wizard of Homesickness.

When I asked him to call his sister he said, "Tell her to text me." Seems the college experience was maturing him, nurturing a manly preference for minimalist communication.

The evening before the last day of camp John prepped the car and mapped his route. He never fell into his typical deep sleep snore that night, and woke at five the next morning for the three-and-a-half hour drive. On the way home, they shared the cab of the truck with a 9-foot wing span glider, which had earned Zander an A. Once home, John wanted a demonstration, but the Styrofoam structure didn't fly as well in the cul-de-sac as it had on the sprawling campus lawns. The deconstruction and reconstruction had altered its delicate balance, rendering it nothing more than a bulky memento. But the opposite was true for us. With my son home, our family was recalibrated. We had sailed past the mark of success and built confidence for the next challenge. Together, our symmetry was restored—at least until the next test.

That night, at my son's request, we had broccoli for dinner.

Over 40 in a
Botox World

Stuff I Learned at My 40th Birthday Party

I THREW MYSELF A BIG PARTY FOR MY fortieth birthday. We had an 80s Prom theme because apparently my development arrested some time after Madonna's third single went platinum. Also, I wanted a good excuse to tease my hair beyond recognition and lacquer it into place with aerosol hairspray. I wasn't alone. We had a great time channeling our inner Wang Chung. We lit up the dance floor old school style. In addition to celebrating this milestone date on the calendar in over-the-top style, I learned a few things.

The DJ is not always right, but usually he is.

Even if you think you have awesome taste in retro 80s music, and awesome taste in friends who think *Prince* and *Tears For Fears* are like totally rad, the era can get tiresome. Sometimes people just want the kind of music played at wedding receptions. Listen to your DJ. Tip him well.

Pretend magic wands actually work.

It is never too late to be a fairy princess. All you need are sparkly streamers and pixie dust.

Aqua Net is a process.

When I was in high school, I left my can of hairspray at home, but how I made it through the school day without re-application is a mystery. At the party we used cans of Aqua Net in as table décor, so I always had one at the ready when my hair started to fall.

With flash photography, there is no such thing as too much makeup.

I would like to embrace the natural look but that would be a lie. Even in a daylight non-party situation I want makeup. I love makeup. I need makeup. The more pictures, the more makeup. No better excuse to wear too much of it than planning an evening around the decade of excess.

Balloon arches make everything better.

Sometimes they can break a fall, but don't count on it.

Social media is fun, if you're careful.

When you invite a bunch of people who own cameras and Facebook accounts to your party, don't drink—especially that purple thing your alcoholic friend hands you, and then hands you again, and once more in case you accidentally dumped it into the fake plant. If you choose to imbibe: deny,

deny, deny. (On second thought, with all that hairspray and makeup, maybe a few more drinks would have made for better pictures.)

If you want it how you want it, you have to do it yourself.
Some people help you, some don't, but ultimately your happiness is up to you.

Some girls are still mean.
Some things that happened in high school will still happen, no matter how many milestone birthdays you have. Some girls will say mean things in the bathroom, right before they eat your birthday cake. But the older you get, the less you care.

Hot is hot, even when it's not.
It's always nice to be called hot, even if the boy who says it is younger than the boy who took you to your actual prom over twenty years ago. And not hot.

Tiaras rule.
The most important thing I learned at the party—and from turning forty in general—is this: It's a fine line, but you must learn to wear the tiara as long as you can get away with it, and not a minute longer.

Pass Me the Push-Up

EARLY ON, WHEN IT LOOKED LIKE MY breasts might actually surpass an A-cup, I feared they'd turn out like my mother's. So did she. From their tentative first showing in the fourth grade, when my above average body weight triggered early puberty, my mother lamented.

"I just hope you don't get the hang-down kind," she said. "Maybe you'll be lucky." She shook her head. "But everyone else in our family has hang-down titties."

Turned out our fear was unfounded. Even gravity needs something to work with. My elementary school fortune was pretty much all I'd ever get, and for a while that was okay. I hadn't yet been exposed to enough *James Bond* and *National Lampoon* movies to know that the desired look was perky, plump, and jiggly. As a kid I just wanted my mother to stop saying titties.

There was less pressure in the 8os. Fake boobs were for centerfolds, trophy wives, and certain "cocktail waitresses."

Even Victoria's Secret models were flatter back then. Surgery to increase breast size still seemed extreme. But things turned in the 90s, when breast augmentation became an appropriate gift from parents to daughters on a sixteenth birthday. According to the American Society of Plastic Surgeons (if a Nip/Tuck doctor's word can be trusted) a quarter of a million women get implants every year. The procedure is so affordable that every bank teller, sales clerk, and Denny's waitress can get a set for $99 down and five years of monthly installments.

Like a Hyundai.

It's not that I never wanted larger breasts, but actually getting cut open in order to have them never seemed—well, rational. Still, some of my friends have encouraged me to have my breasts done. (Especially those who see me at the lake.) I have resisted for several reasons. First there is the risk of going under anesthesia. I'd hate to burden my husband with explaining how Mommy had a heart attack on the table because she wanted men to look at her chest.

Aside from my exaggerated fear of death-by-facemask, there is a more practical reason I opt out of saline or silicon: They don't last forever. This I learned when a forty-something friend told me that she was having hers replaced. *Replaced.* Like old tires or a worn-out A/C unit, breast implants need to be swapped out at regular intervals. At most they last maybe twenty years. Getting your breasts done at forty means facing another surgery at sixty, and then again at eighty. Because who doesn't want to be hot in the halls of the nursing home?

And then there's the cost. Easy payment plan or no, breasts aren't cheap. I was talking to a friend at her garage sale.

"You have GOT to get these," she said, hoisting her new appendages up with a squeeze. "Save up. It's only five grand."

Meanwhile she's selling her old padded bikini tops to make the payment.

I can get a nice underwire with strategically placed foam, water, or silicone inserts at Walmart for $12.99. That's without a coupon. My strategy stands the test of time, as proven by my great-grandmother, who wore "cheaters" in her bra until she died at 93. It took a while for me to wise up to this less drastic approach. For years I resisted padded bras in favor of upper body integrity. I reserved artificially enhanced bras for special occasions: Anniversaries, New Year's Eve, slutty Halloween costumes. Then I got over it. I bought a few push-up bras and started experimenting. I watched men turn stupid in a way my A-cups had never inspired. I was ogled; I liked it. Then I took off my pretend boobies and went for a run. Since then I have learned that the padded push-up is the best of all worlds. I can be ballerina-flat in a tank top one minute, and busting out like a corseted stripper the next.

Ladies, if you doubt the power of a push-up bra, take yourself down to the nearest discount retailer for a bra and a lacy camisole to accent your new faux cleavage. Then go somewhere—anywhere—and observe human behavior.

Men, you are being deceived. Enjoy.

If only I had bought those enhanced bikini tops from my friend, I'd be ready for lake season.

Who Peed on My Yoga Mat?

I DON'T WANT TO BRAG, BUT ON A GOOD day I can almost put my foot behind my head. That's how long I've been practicing yoga. For years I have been driving halfway across town at an inconvenient hour to some mint green room with a lavender candle, and a stack of Mexican blankets in the back. I love taking class, but I'm rarely motivated to bust out a crow or a sun salutation on my own.

Frustrated with my need for someone else to tell me when to breathe, I recently set out to cultivate a more personal practice, a home practice. I embarked on a six-week program of daily poses, to be attempted first thing each morning, long before my regular instructor had cued up the pan flute playlist.

On day one, I got up all bright-eyed and ohm-y-tailed and progressed through the prescribed series of poses, congratulating myself on my ability to resist the temptation of the snooze bar and my fortitude in assuming the positions without external direction.

Yay, Me!

At the end of the strenuous postures came the time of relaxation. Savasana is also known as the Dead Man, or Corpse Pose. This is the best part of yoga practice as it consists entirely of lying on your mat doing nothing more strenuous than being aware of your breath. Even without an instructor's prompts, I was nailing this pose.

Unfortunately, it fell at just about the time the rest of the family's alarm clocks chimed. This did not contribute to any sense of inner peace, as I imagined the kids finding me there in the hall, laid out on my mat like—well, like a corpse. I calculated the likelihood of their stepping on my head just because they could. Then I reminded myself to let those distractions go, to stay in the moment, focus on my breath, and whatever else that barefooted, do-ragged yogi on the cover of the book advised. But his Eastern wisdom was drowned out by thoughts of the morning chaos soon to come:

Did you sign my slip?

Where are my jeans?

Why is this milk yellow?

How was a girl to relax when so many demands loomed? And more important: what was that smell? I had to find a way to clear it all out. My stillness was at stake, and I'm nothing without personal tranquility—plus three cups of coffee. It's a miracle I was even awake at that hour, let alone that my senses were working. Especially smell. And this one was not good. All my downward dogging must have heated up the mat, releasing some kind of toxic resin.

I should really get an organic mat.

Or, you could just wash this one.

Excuse me? What, am I talking to myself now? Can't you see I'm trying to meditate here?

What is that smell? Is that pee?

Oh, please, Can we focus, for like five more minutes?

Seriously. It's pee. I'm telling you.

Don't be ridiculous. Why would anyone pee on our mat?

Why would anyone put a salami sandwich in the dishwasher? Why would anyone freeze a spider? Why would anyone eat oysters from a can? We live among savages.

Just then, amid the senseless mental chatter, a stronger, louder call to action:

Serenity NOW! cried my inner George Costanza.

Maybe he knew who peed on my yoga mat.

I had to laugh. Up before dawn to steal time for an ancient practice, on a urine-soaked mat, and I am interrupted by *Seinfeld*? I must have needed the yoga more than I thought. I laughed some more. And then, in a moment of divine insight I remembered. Yes, that's right. It was me.

That one time?

In hot flow class?

When my warrior busted over into the next girl's mat?

And it was so funny?

I peed on my yoga mat.

(Note to self: Set up a calendar reminder for Kegels.)

From now on I'll stick to the spendy studio with the "suggested donation" basket. At least there I only have to worry about strangers stepping on my head, and they clean the communal mats every day. Even if I pee on them.

From Pillow to Pedometer in
6 Easy Steps

I TEXTED HER BEFORE BED: RUN. 6:30?

Two weeks of vacation had left me bloated on Brie and wine. I needed to sweat, and I wanted company. The response came back immediately. Something about getting home late from a business dinner, having a presentation due early, she *totally* wanted to run—like really, really, really—but she couldn't.

No worries. I'm a big girl. I didn't need the knowledge that my friend was waiting in the dark to pry my soft ass out of bed. I could run all by myself. Besides, my husband was leaving town in the morning. Instead of dashing off for an early jog while he was still in the shower, I'd say a proper goodbye and exercise later. You know what this was?

A BLESSING IN DISGUISE!

(I had to shout that last part to drown out the voices

telling me that I know damn well that it will be too hot to run by the time I finish toast and coffee and "goodbye.")

The next morning, after hitting the snooze a few times. It went down like this:

1. "Hey, Babe, let's have coffee." First mistake. Who runs after drinking coffee? Not me. I'm not willing to pee myself in the name of fitness. For funny anecdotes, sure, but not merely for shapelier thighs.

2. Oh, look! Laundry! I should totally fold that load before I leave. I find it's important to have certain chores witnessed by my family. Helps to back up the occasional tirade: "I slave away all day for you people! Where is the gratitude?"

3. I'm not yet in running clothes when I kiss my husband goodbye, shut the door, and notice a neat stack of bills on the desk. That looks fun! Compared to a 3-mile run, car payments are delightful. But, no. I'm strong. I will resist the lure of the bills and hit the pavement. Just as soon as I dust the decorative items I have acquired for just such an occasion.

4. When I finally make it to the closet, I argue with myself about whether or not the black of my tank matches the black of my running skirt. I should really get some new socks. By the way, hello sock drawer! Do you need organizing, Little Buddy?

5. After a pre-run insurance pee, I notice the ring around the toilet bowl. It's not the first time I've seen it. Since vacation, with catching up on work and unpacking and stocking the pantry and all that laundry, I haven't gotten to the bathrooms. Suddenly I'm craving a hit of Comet. I may need help.

6. Dragging myself away from the scrubbing bubbles, I emerge, victorious, on my front steps wearing unmatched socks and a Band-Aid on my heel. Today, I run! Cueing up the Pandora channel, I prepare for the inevitable agony. The pain will pay off later when I attack the carne asada tacos with guacamole and cheese. Maybe even Brie. I will suffer no remorse as I watch my friend eat salad with vinegar dressing.

My September Issues

EVERY SEPTEMBER I BUY FASHION magazines. This is going to be the year, I think, that I get a real wardrobe, really pay attention to what's in style, rid my closet of everything that doesn't make me feel fabulous. It starts before the thick issues hit newsstands. Early in August I start looking forward to fall's flattering colors and coverage. My standard fashion inferiority complex steps aside in favor of hope. This time, with the right motivation and resources, I too can master the skills of selecting, accessorizing, and combining high and low.

This particular obsession must have its roots in years of being the new girl in school almost every September. If only I could get the clothes right, everything else would fall into place. That never happened, and, sadly, my fashion deficiency did not end in high school. The closest I've ever come to chic were Anna Wintour bangs. Turns out those don't flatter just anyone.

My problem is that I don't enjoy shopping, not for clothes, anyway. Give me a grocery cart and an expanse of peaceful rows and I'm like a Zen monk tending a sand garden. But shopping for clothing is almost always painful. Unless I'm in a mood. And then the task is uncharacteristically exhilarating and I come home with bags full of crap I will either return or hang in my closet only to donate months or years later to a charitable organization so some less fortunate woman can figure out what to do with a polka dot bolero jacket.

This year, as I dutifully cleaned and organized my closet, I was able to part with the seventeen-year-old metallic cro-cheted Gap sweater. However, the suede jeans made the cut, if only because they have to put in their time. After cleaning out my closet, I pored over the September issues, marking pages with fashions that might work with my body type and coloring. Also, they had to fit my budget and be just as com-fortable standing in line at Walmart as they are lounging over a $16,000 chaise lounge. And of course, no article of clothing is allowed to make my butt look big.

This year I met a magazine editor who introduced me to an extreme wardrobe challenge. In this exercise in utilization and editing, you wear every item in your closet, moving from left to right. Each day you have to figure out how to wear the next-up item or get rid of it. This is very different than my usual strategy of wearing the same pair of jeans until they disintegrate off my body into a pile of indigo lint. Like most women, I'd love to have more clothes. But I also realize that I probably have enough of them already, if I'd just wear them all.

My clothes don't play well together. I've had so many different clothing needs in my adult life that I haven't had the opportunity to build a cohesive wardrobe. In college I started collecting suits and other accoutrements of the conservative CPA image required at the Big Six accounting firm that hired me my senior year. The bastion of navy suits, hose and pumps was abruptly dismissed when the firm adopted a business casual dress code complete with confusing genres of khaki. The only thing more difficult to define than business casual is cocktail casual, but at least that comes with drinks.

After cubicle life came the stay-at-home mom phase of getting drooled and shat upon. Then came a stint in home party sales where my attire needed to look put together while allowing me to haul crates to and from my car over uneven yards scattered with Little Tykes, trikes, and the occasional flock of chickens. Now I live in yoga pants and flip flops, unless I'm meeting with a consulting client, or chatting on the morning news. You can understand why I have issues. Some days it's a wonder I get dressed at all.

Standing in my clean and organized closet with stack of magazines and a strategy, I realized that I owned none of the top ten wardrobe essentials of the season. Where was the camel-colored leather vest? The electric blue high-heeled oxfords? Where were all the zipper tanks? Not in my closet.

Another September and I am still no Anna Wintour. Defeated, I pulled out a white t-shirt and my trusty frayed jeans. This combination is not stylish and it won't make me popular, but it was clean and didn't make my butt look big. And it's better than leaving the house naked, which would create a much worse set of September issues.

At least I've learned to stay away from bangs.

To Tox or Not To Tox

I'VE BEEN THINKING ABOUT BOTOX lately. A lot. Mostly due to the line next to my left eyebrow that no longer responds to my "rub it out" method of wrinkle removal. Maybe the barely perceptible line has been bugging me because most of my friends are younger than I am. Maybe it's because I just got back from California where everyone is injected in all the right places. Maybe it's because I spend all day online where people are digitally smooth. Maybe we can blame Skype—every moment of a phone call staring into a mirror. Who thought that was a good idea?

Worrying about the line won't make it go away. In fact, maybe if I didn't worry at all, I wouldn't have any lines! Maybe I could attain some higher level of inner peace so I wouldn't make the face that causes the line in the first place. Or at least I wouldn't want the injections. But that would never work. Even if I mysteriously transformed into the picture of tranquility, I would still have to use the computer and go out in the sun. Hello, squinty lines.

I've got a decision to make: To tox or not to tox. It's not a big deal. It's not like I haven't done it before.

I hadn't planned it, but once, just before I turned forty, I had a weak moment at the dermatologist's office. When the esthetician finished shaping my eyebrows, I asked if she could give me more of an arch. No, she said. It wouldn't look right.

"You know what you'd really like?" she asked.

I couldn't tell if she was really excited to tell me, or surprised, or if her battery might be shorting out. Like all the women who work at the skin doctor/facial rejuvenation clinic/spa, this one had been plumped and sanded so much that she resembled an American Girl doll version of herself. Occupational perks.

"What would I like?" I asked.

"Just a tiny bit of Botox," she pointed a wooden stick just above my brow. "Right there."

"For my eyebrows? People do that?"

"You'd only need a few units."

She explained how disabling the tiny muscle just above the arch of my brows would cause them to lift, ever so slightly. It would be subtle. I would love it. And of course, if I opted for just a few units on either side of my forehead, I may as well do in between the brows, too, right? Oh, but yes! It was all very impulse buy and I needed to decide quickly as the technician who administered the Botox was extremely busy. Actually, I was lucky because she just so happened to have an opening. If I didn't catch her now, it could be months before I had another opportunity to take a needle to my face.

Months.

"You know it's not really poison, right," said the tech ten minutes later as I sat holding a cool gel pack on my face in preparation for the shot.

"Oh, yeah, of course," I lied.

"It's just a protein," she said. "It's inactive,"

Sure. It has TOX in the name; it's harmless. Despite having recently watched a particularly horrifying prime time news special where some nice couple got a non-poisonous injection that paralyzed and nearly killed them both, I wasn't actually worried about the health effects. I was worried that once I started I wouldn't be able to stop. I'd turn into one of those aging actresses they use to sell the Stars Without Makeup issue of the National Enquirer, my face all pulled and pinched, perpetually shocked. I'd spend my kids' college fund on mini-lifts, moving on to the Full Monty: the tummy tuck-boob job combo. Not that there's anything wrong with that.

Fear didn't stop me, however. I took my fourteen units and got on with the day. That afternoon and the next my eyelids felt heavy. A few days later they lifted and I became unable to make a mean face. Well, I could, but I really had to try. Still, it was subtle. So much so that no one noticed. When it wore off, I didn't go back for the next notch on my Botox club punch card.

I don't really need Botox. If I discontinue any form of concentration the line might not go away, but it might not get any deeper either. If I get some better sunglasses I won't have to squint so much. And if my family would start taking out the trash I could quit making that face. And yet, here I am again. It's two years later and there's that line on my lip.

In the parking lot I see just how successful my dermatologist has become. Cadillacs, Mercedes, and Jaguars, the preferred transportation of trophy wives everywhere. This is going to be expensive. Inside is the paradise I remember: Soothing blue walls, a lamp lit glow, soft botanicals on the walls, expressionless young women at reception, and furniture that cost more than my car. With regular visits my skin could become as sumptuous and touchable as the chenille, velvet, and silk surfaces surrounding me. I watch a tall woman checking out in front of me. I can't see her face, but her clothes look old. She has wrinkly elbows, a flat ass, and the posture of osteoporosis. Syringes can't fix everything. A sign on the desk displays the Wi-Fi password. The Keurig calls to me. I wonder if they would let me stay here and work all day. Every day.

I want to be above it all, too good for unnatural enhancements. I want to age gracefully, not squander precious disposable income on vanity. But I also want that line on my lip to go away. I'm no better than any other facially desensitized woman. When you think about it, the Botox keeps me grounded, brings my righteousness down a notch. It's not vice in those vials; it's liquid humility. As I recover from the sting of four painful pricks to my upper lip, the tech tells me I'll dribble when I try to drink from a straw for the first few days. She does not dispose of the syringe in the medically safe receptacle on the counter, but rather casually leaves it on the windowsill. That can't be good.

Injections complete, I ask for recommendations on skin care.

"We need to start focusing on anti-aging," the tech says.

Really? They teach you that kind of communication in pretend doctor school, or are you trying to be mean?

"Let me ask you something," she says. "Do you mind putting different things on your face or are you one of these people who likes to keep it simple?"

"I just had you shoot poison into my lip," I tell her. "I'll do what it takes."

"You'd be surprised," she says. But I wouldn't, actually. It makes perfect sense to me that people who inject toxins, plastics, and their own ass fat into their faces would insist upon the appearance of a minimalist approach.

As I leave I think I should tell my husband what I've done, just in case I get some tox-induced neuro-disorder requiring immediate medical attention. But I won't. To tox or not to tox is a personal decision. Besides, it will be obvious. Why else would I stop making that face?

Losers Always Win

IN THE EARLY DAYS OF OUR RELATIONSHIP, my husband played soccer. I'm sure Victoria Beckham will back me up when I say soccer players are hot. John loved the game for its own sake, while I, being chronically bad at any sport involving a ball, just wanted to work out. I tried every aerobic exercise fad there was. If there was a VHS made for it during the 80s and 90s, I did it. While John was never the gym rat I was, we consummated our commitment by joining a health club together. He wore his soccer jersey and I sported a fluorescent thong over black biker shorts. We were extra sexy. And in shape. We even played walleyball. Top that.

However, as men often do in the courting phase, my beloved was only pretending. He didn't really enjoy working out. Over the years we've belonged to half a dozen health clubs, and while I kept busy boxing, belly dancing, and step aerobicising myself into superior bone density, the most consistent thing about my husband's routine has been his line, "I go to the gym once a month—to pay the bill." If he'd logged as many workouts as he has repetitions of that tired joke, I'd be sleeping with a romance novel cover model.

But I'm not.

John has long since passed the appropriate age to run swearing up and down a soccer field, but a few years ago he took up the sport again. And by this I mean he played a game with the guys after work. It ended with some mumbling about pain and "…every muscle in my body." Regardless, something had made him feel thirty again. With his new youthful delusion came sprints down a field made for younger men. It was longer than he remembered. And more painful. Can you say Achilles tendonitis?

When I finally convinced him to see a doctor about it, he received this warning:

"You'd better start shopping for a good cardiologist."

Turns out his foot wasn't the only thing out of shape. Lucky for him, losing weight is trendy. Just before Christmas last year, everyone at the office made plans for their annual weight loss competition. They had even cut a deal with a gym to get a group discount. Not two miles from our house is a flagship facility we'll call Biggest Gym Ever. According to the guy in the muscle-hugging spandex who tried to sell us a membership last year, it is the largest Biggest Gym Ever in the world. Though he baited us with executive locker rooms and personal training—all free with 30-year fixed rate minimum monthly auto-draft—we declined, opting instead to spend our hard-earned cash on running shoes and lunch from greasy taco joints.

But there was that discount…

My husband waffled for a month. "I don't know. Do you think I should?"

"Will you go?" I asked

"I should."

"But will you?"

He half shrugged. "It's fifteen dollars off." As if the price of a meat lover's pizza could really be the determining factor in his longevity.

I tried everything—appeals to his vanity, morbid talk of cardiac events, and even an offer to get up at five in the morning and join him at the gym. When he still couldn't decide, I reminded him that there are always hot girls at Biggest Gym Ever.

Sold.

This was mid-December. "So," I said, "you getting up early tomorrow?"

"Of course not," he said. "I can't work out *now*."

"Why not?"

"I'm in training." His expression told me this statement made sense to him. Relationship experts will tell you that communication is the key to a lasting relationship. Nearly twenty years in, I can state with confidence that they are wrong. A lot of things are more important—sex, steady paychecks, and division of labor to name a few. However, I have learned to communicate entire paragraphs with just one look, which I did. So he explained.

"I can't lose weight now—not *before* the weigh-in!" His goal was to gain ten pounds before the first of the year—before the weigh-in—and then lose the extra pounds quickly and take home the prize. And we wonder what's wrong with Corporate America.

John lost his training weight. Then he gained it back, misplaced it again on the treadmill, and finally found it at Sonic. He did not win, or lose, as it were.

As for the gym? He still goes.

At least once a month.

Adventures
& Advice

Car Trouble, Vacation Style

THE RENTAL FORD FIESTA DID not approve of the warm weather.

"Um...why is this car overheating?" my husband asked, as if this were some innocuous question and not a significant foreteller of doom. Didn't matter. When it comes to cars I barely know what overheating means. To me, cars should just run. I want my involvement to begin with the key and end with the payment. My husband's face changed. "There's something seriously wrong with this car."

He pulled onto the side of the highway just as the little party of a car died. Not the ideal ending to a day spent in carefree exploration of the Mallorcan countryside. Yes, Mallorca, as in Spain. We had been there a week visiting the sites of my husband's idyllic childhood summers spent swimming in the shadow of the cliffs of Valdemossa, la Costa Norte. We had wanted a day of picturesque, unplugged escape. All urgent orders and imperative emails would be waiting when we got back. We'd wanted to disconnect from the real and virtual problems of our non-vacation lives, linked instead to the living, breathing people we loved most. Which is why we had left our phones at the hotel.

Never mind that phones make outgoing calls.

At least my husband speaks the language. My ability to communicate consists of "Muy bonita!" "Mas vino, por favor" and "Wi-Fi? You have Wi-Fi?"

"Do you want me to warm up my hitchhiking thumb?" my daughter asked, giddy at the prospect of adventure in a foreign land. When she was two years old she stuck her finger in a gin and tonic, licked it, and grinned. Since then we have known she tends toward the Party Girl. We have anticipated disputes over boys snuck in and out of windows, and worried about college classes spent sleeping it off. Maybe it's our fault for getting that keg for her first birthday barbecue. I made a mental note to instill in her the proper fear of strange men and box vans, and returned to the panic at hand.

But only for a moment because just as soon as I started to sweat, I remembered who I married. The engineer, the handyman, fixer of all things. My husband would roll up his sleeves and pop the hood right there on the shoulder of the highway, mere inches from the semi-trucks and smart cars whizzing by. He'd tighten some metal thingy or insert a magical fluid, possibly fashion a new auto part out of gum wrappers and empty Fanta cans, and we'd be on our way. I married well.

Maybe my optimism was more powerful than I knew, because John did not have to pull out the MacGyver moves.

Miraculously, after a few minutes, he tried the ignition and the car started.

Back in motion, I took in the vistas and let my mind wander. It had been a wonderful week. Waking early to jog along the marina walkway, with its ancient stucco homes and paint-chipped sail boats, drinking good wine on the cheap, and watching my kids flip a switch from children to teenagers. Our summer in Spain, that's how this would be remembered. We soon exited the main highway for the country road that led back to the quaint fishing village, loaves of bread, and rounds of Brie whose calories wouldn't count until we got back home.

Life was good.

Then the car stopped again.

This time we pulled over behind a tour bus that had also broken down. John got out and popped the lid while the bus driver approached. The cranky old Spaniard motioned to the engine and said something that I interpreted as a grave determination. A few minutes later John asked for all the water bottles in the car. The kids and I watched as he poured them into the insatiable radiator. Either this was going to work, or we'd be awfully thirsty on our 20-mile walk back to the hotel.

John and the bus driver soon diagnosed the problem. The bad news: There was a hole in the radiator. The good news: There was a phone in the old man's pocket. We used it to call the rental car company.

The old man spoke English, but apparently did not understand automated responses. "She says 'Push one.' What is 'Push one'?"

After my charming husband managed to convey the message that we were stranded on the side of the road, he started talking to the other guy—the Ecuadorian. Ecuador, you may know, is in South America, and is a very long way from the European vacation destination of Mallorca, which is not known for abundant employment opportunities. So when el Bus Driver told us in broken English that he had come to the island from halfway around the world because he "heard there were jobs," I had to assume there was a death squad on his ass.

It didn't help when he started asking how much we paid for airfare and the particulars of our hotel. I knew immediately that he wanted to kill us. My own mother did a fine job of making me aware of the dangers of strange men. I tried to be optimistic, anyway. Instead of imagining my children sold into sex slavery and my husband parted out for meat, I focused on the sound of goat bells tinkling as the goats grazed in the late afternoon sunlight. I savored the sounds of a confused rooster who crowed at this inappropriate hour. Stuck or not, the place was still tranquil. I wanted to take a picture, but I hesitated to display the expensive new camera we bought for the trip. Even if he didn't abduct us, Scarface might have wanted a token of our appreciation for his crack automotive advice. In fact, that probably wasn't the car rental agency they dialed earlier, but accomplices who now knew that a fresh batch of clueless Americans was ready for pick up.

The kids were fine. They had brought their sustenance

and were perfectly content playing Nintendo DS in the back-seat.

At least I was free of the small talk. John patiently listened to what I assume was a carefully crafted life story of the bus driver—one that left out drug deals gone wrong, a narrow escape through the jungle, and his counterfeit passport. I understand enough Spanish to get by, but I know nothing of the language spoken by locals on the island. My husband does, though, and he uses it. While I don't comprehend the words, I do speak body language. The bus driver's said:

This car is dead. You are screwed. Ain't no rental company picking you up before sunrise.

Paraphrasing, of course.

Thankfully, the rental company did show up, in a timely fashion, and before any of our critical organs were removed for sale on the Ecuadorian black market. We made it back to the room, where my phone sat on the dresser, fully charged, and never to be more than six inches from my twitchy fingers again.

Take Me Out to the Ball Game

I HAVE BEEN TO APPROXIMATELY HALF a dozen baseball games in my life, always for reasons other than watching a baseball game. In the mid-90s the objective was to get a job at a Big Six consulting firm. It worked. Or maybe the job offer was due to my ability to feign interest in audit reports and IRS Code. In '98 I attended a few games to celebrate my husband's work on the retractable roof at Seattle's Safeco Field.

A decade has passed and I've returned to baseball, for an end-of season hockey party, naturally. Four years ago, the spot where we sit was grazing land for Hereford stocker calves. You can still see cattle in the distance. This is not the major leagues. This is Arkansas. Rumor has it that a prominent local televangelist pulled support—and that of his deep-pocketed friends—when the team wouldn't back down from selling alcohol at the games.

They built the place anyway, and the liquor is cheap.

LELA DAVIDSON

As a casual observer of the national pastime, there are many things I do not understand.

Mascots

We start the evening with pizza and awards for the kids. Then, after three men water down the dirt, but before the first pitch, my children and their teammates—all in their hockey jerseys—parade onto the field, where they are met by the Northwest Arkansas Naturals' mascot, Strike—a Sasquatch. Hardly the mythical Big Foot of my Pacific Northwest childhood, but we could have done worse. Here in Springdale, home to Tyson Foods, "Naturals" almost didn't beat the second place contender, "Thunder Chickens." Then again, a chicken running around like a chicken with its head cut off might have been more entertaining. And of course, that's why we're here—to be entertained, family style. It's the reason we have promised the kids we'll stay until the end of the game, in case there are fireworks.

Snacks

My husband informs me that we are sitting in the section where you could get hit by a foul ball. But only from the lefties. Small comfort. I have more pressing problems, like how to consume hotdogs, cotton candy, nachos, funnel cakes, pretzels, and enormous bowls of soft serve. It's all about pacing. Meanwhile the guy next to us has chosen peanuts, and he's tossing the shells on the concrete at our feet.

"Is that normal?" I ask my husband.

He shrugs. "Yeah, it's what you do. It's baseball."

I send my husband for beer. The 32-ounce Miller High Life costs only seventy-five cents more than the 24-ounce Bud Light tall boy. No contest. Plus, Miller is the "Champagne of Beers." All we need are baseball bat shaped flutes bearing the facsimile signature of a favorite double-A player who may someday make it to the *Kansas City Royals*.

He brings back a sack of peanuts. He demonstrates the proper technique, and soon the shells surround my feet.

Meanwhile, my kids are desperately trying to get on the Jumbotron.

I really, really need that beer.

Stats

By the sixth inning, all but the most devoted fans have lost interest in the actual game. I join my husband where he is talking to the other hockey dads above our section. I have heard all their jokes before, so I am half paying attention to their conversation when I notice two women in their seventies sitting in the handicapped accessible seating, bearing clipboards with attached pens. When I introduce myself I find out they're recording stats. These sisters have been season ticket holders since the team moved here from Wichita three years ago. They don't bet on the games, but they do record every single, double, and RBI. The devoted fans also collect players' autographs on their season programs, and well as other memorabilia, like the plastic baseball hat-shaped ice cream cups.

"If you get a silver Sharpie, it shows up real good," one of them tells me.

When I ask what they did for fun before we built what I refer to as the baseball "stadium," they don't seem to remember. They are also too kind to correct me. Even I know it's called a ballpark. But I forgot. Blame it on the champagne of beers.

Maybe the preacher was right.

Innings, Especially the Seventh

Back in my seat, I eat the rest of the peanuts, dropping the shells onto the concrete in front of me. Something tells me the Scorecard Sisters would not approve. Soon, everyone gets up.

"Why are we standing?" I ask a friend.

"It's the seventh inning." When I don't respond, she shakes her head. "This is the seventh inning stretch. It is done at every game at every baseball park across America. How can you not know that?"

It's not like I'd never heard of the seventh inning stretch; I just didn't realize it was a regular thing.

During the eighth inning, our Naturals break out the heavy theatrics. The head coach puts on a show of anger at a call. Something about the player being hit with a ball. Chests are thrust and dirt is kicked. Other than that, there are no fireworks, we lose, and I won't find the gum on the bottom of my purse until the next morning.

I still don't understand baseball. That's not going to change. And while I'll never be a season ticket holder, I will be back—if only for the cheap beer and funnel cakes.

Advice for Beautiful Wives

Dear Lela,

My friends think it's weird that my husband is on Facebook so much, but he's just a very social person. Besides, I like it when he posts sweet updates like, "Having lunch with my beautiful wife." How can I tell my friends to let it go without coming across as a total bi-atch?

Happily Married to a Great Guy

Dear Happily,

First of all, before you even finish reading this response, call up every single friend who has warned you about your husband's Facebooking ways and invite her to dinner at the nicest restaurant you can afford. I'll wait.

You back?

Okay, now listen to me very carefully. While I know nothing of your husband's possible social media skankery, I suggest you go ahead and call the best divorce lawyer you can afford. According to a married male friend of mine, the possible meanings of "Having lunch with my beautiful wife" include:

- Boy, my marriage feels a bit shaky. Better prop it up with an affirming status update.
- Boy, my marriage is on the rocks but I don't want anyone to know yet. Better put on a good show on Facebook.
- In case nobody's noticed, my wife is really hot, which means I managed to snag a hottie, which means I must be hot, which means other women among my Facebook friends ought to be hot for me.
- If I say on Facebook that my wife is beautiful, she'll be more likely to have sex with me tonight.
- Having lunch with my beautiful wife.

As you can see, there is at least a twenty percent probability that your husband's status is honest and without motive. I'm sure there are plenty of men who sincerely want to express their devotion via the newsfeed. Others simply don't know what to do on Facebook and since their wives are on that damn thing all day anyway, why not score a few points? However, it's been my experience that husbands (and wives) who feel the need to make a public profession of their good marital fortune usually have something to prove and/or atone for.

I could be wrong. Maybe you're accustomed to being reminded upon waking how gorgeous you are. Your husband might be one of those appreciative types who thanks you for washing his jeans. Perhaps you get a big pat on the back for every orgasm you assist. And maybe you reciprocate all this praise and appreciation. Well, bravo to you! I live in a different normal. In my world polite is a death sentence. Common courtesy consists of "Do you want to use the bathroom first?" And any compliment beyond "Damn, your ass looks good in those" is grounds for suspicion.

Your man may be the exception, but it sounds like your girlfriends know better. Believe them, and spring for the top shelf liquor at that dinner.

Terror in the Corn Maze

FOR YEARS MY FAMILY TRIED TO get me into a corn maze. They finally succeeded on the pretense of a Girl Scout outing. My daughter cared less about the maze than the accumulation of badges, and she'd already picked out a spot on her green vest for the gigantic ear of corn that symbolized overcoming the challenge. So, after having suffered the actual corn maze, I would be rewarded with the monumental task of affixing the badge to the sash. When she started Girl Scouts we had to choose between the sash and the vest, which held more badges. I'm an optimist, so I bought the sash hoping she'd lose interest after the first year. However, it didn't look like I'd get my wish. The girl would do anything for a badge. She was so competitive I wouldn't have been surprised if she got the Gold Medal for crocheting a scarf out of yarn she made herself from sheep she raised in the back yard.

On this corn maze thing, she was taking hostages.

Every year before this my family asked me to take them to a corn maze, and every year I found an excuse to say no to that particular brand of terrifying "family fun." No good can come from getting lost amid stalks. It's not that I don't like corn. Creamed corn, corn on the cob, corn fritters, corn bread, candy corn, cornstarch, corn chips. Love them all. I just don't understand what is supposed to be fun about getting lost on purpose. This phobia is not my fault. I blame *Children of the Corn*. Or any other horror film. What would a slasher flick be without corn syrup? I also believe that corn-cob violence during October and November is greatly underreported. It's a scary food group.

One might get lost in corn, never to be seen or heard from again. This year, one unfortunate family made national headlines for their panicked 9-1-1 call from the belly of a corn beast. As darkness fell, they were unable to find their way out of a corn maze. This is supposed to be a crop, not wholesome autumn entertainment. But that bit of handy news came too late for me this year. Even if it hadn't, there was the badge at stake.

Off we went, venturing deep into the Ozark mountains, which are really just hills. Broken down shacks, trailers with corrugated green plastic roofing, and rusted everything made up the scenery on the way to the corn maze. This did little for my confidence in the type of people who ran the place. Would they employ state of the art maze GPS tracking? Not likely. Would they kill us and sell our organs? Perhaps. On the drive in I imagined a whole cottage industry of human spleens harvested among the stalks. We passed through several towns where the only productive thing a person can do is to leave. In one such town was a filling station (that is what they are called in these parts) advertising buffalo meat for sale.

"Oh, sure," I said, "that's what they call it. Just don't get lost in the corn." Sorry, people of the hills, but it's not a stretch to think that those who would pickle and eat the foot of a pig might not be squeamish about your tender bicep flesh.

No worries. I had a plan. And a phone with GPS.

A couple miles from the corn maze, just when I thought I'd found an app that might keep me safe—or at least my next of kin notified of my whereabouts—I lost my signal. The lightning started just as we turned onto the gravel road, and continued to provide dramatic ambiance as we approached the entrance, which happened to be a cemetery. Not a normal cemetery, with smooth cut rocks and tidy rows, but a creepy country ordeal complete with a gnarly old tree and a barbed wire fence. Just in case anyone wanted to break in.

Or out.

"There sure are a lot of people here," my husband said as we pulled into the parking lot.

"That's because they're all lost in the corn maze," I told him. "It's like a roach motel for stupid humans."

My daughter, the sensitive one, said from the back seat. "We're all gonna die!"

I expected to see a crucifix made of corn husks any minute. Instead, there was a sign advertising hayrides and a petting zoo. I believed it housed puppies of families who never came out of the corn.

When we found the rest of the troop, I wondered if the

leader had Thin Mints and Samoas in her fanny pack. You know, in case we weren't murdered right off, but had to survive by our wits, hiding from hungry hillbillies and He Who Walks Behind the Rows.

The fates were with us that day. Shortly after we arrived, the corn maze was closed due to the rain. My fear of corn mazes continued, but I wouldn't have to face it for at least another year. My daughter took a consolation "rainy day" badge that was nearly as large as the corn badge, and just as difficult to sew onto her sash. A few months later she resigned. Any future attempts to convince me to risk my life in rows of corn would not be assisted by the full backing of the Girl Scouts of America. But those crafty corn maze proprietors have come up with a new selling point: going into the maze after dark, with merely a flashlight to guide the way.

Right. I'll be right over, just as soon as I charge my phone and file this Last Will and Testament.

Bleak Friday

SHOPPING IS NOT MY SPORT. And I'm not the girl with red and green bins in the attic begging to bust out the holiday cheer as soon as the turkey cools. For the love of all that is jolly, I still don't know why I decided to drag my sisters-in-law out before dawn the day after Thanksgiving. But I'd never participated in the spectacle and it sounded adventurous. Apparently I am susceptible to glossy flyers and promises of free stuff nobody wants when I buy other stuff nobody wants. The sleek advertising and booming radio announcers bring out my inner door buster. Besides, this could be our thing—Qing, Diana, and me. I hoped Thanksgiving sales had the power to bond us together as the sisters we really weren't. We'd start our own Black Friday tradition.

We woke up on time. That is to say, a few minutes after our husbands ate their final turkey sandwich. However, the day hit a snag when Qing, who is from China—the real China with the strange food and the sketchy restrooms—pulled up at the convenience store.

"What are we doing here?" asked Diana. "There are no sales here."

"You say you want coffee," Qing said. "They have coffee."

Diana explained, as patiently as she could at just after four in the morning, the importance of the right coffee, a triple venti gingerbread vanilla latte with whipped cream and sprinkles, perhaps. Because you can't go into a sporting event unprepared, especially when you are the athlete. Make no mistake, that's exactly what we were. In sweatpants, running shoes, and bad scrunchies, we at least looked the part for the battle ahead. In my zeal to hit the sliding doors running, I actually wore pajamas. In public. They were velour. More of a track suit, if you will. Yes, it was a personal low and I've learned my lesson.

Fortified with caffeine, we hit Target, where I became obsessed with getting not just any air hockey table, but the last air hockey table. And if I could just chase down one of those guys in the red shirts to lift it into my cart, it would be mine.

"The kids like air hockey?" Diana asked.

"They play ice hockey."

Hello? So what if they'd never played air hockey. The idea that we Davidsons could have an air hockey table in our very own house prompted a mental montage of my 1970s childhood. Sure, it wasn't foosball, but still—AIR HOCKEY! And for a mere $49.95. Door bust that, Baby! As far as I was concerned, the day was already a success. "Yep, they are going to love it!" I said, parting the crowds with the huge box hanging over my cart.

Next, we moved on to Old Navy, where they were selling regular Old Navy stuff for regular Old Navy prices. But we had coupons. And those coupons were festive. Caught up in the moment, I bought two fleece blankets. Because they were only five dollars.

Next, we hit a department store. On the way in, Qing asked me to put her wallet in my purse.

"Where's yours?"

"Where's my what?"

"You didn't bring your purse shopping?"

"Why should I bring my purse if all I need is my wallet?"

"Fine, just—walk faster!"

There were picture frames on the line, a set of them. Matching. Once inside I headed to house wares, knocked an elderly woman out of the way, and snagged the last two boxes. Then I gave them to my sisters-in-law. Because I have Christmas spirit. Bonding. See? And all this sunrise shopping is good for America.

Black Friday as we know it has bleak origins, and it's all Thursday's fault. Even though George Washington made Thanksgiving a holiday in 1789, the date wasn't set until 1863, when the holiday was given an official spot on the last Friday of November. This worked out fine until the holiday season of the Great Depression. November 1939 had five Thursdays. Merchants worried that the short window between Thanksgiving and Christmas wouldn't do the economy any favors. But no retailers dared advertise Christmas before

Thanksgiving parades, lest they be smacked in the head by a competitor's turkey carcass. So they convinced Franklin D. Roosevelt to move the date of Thanksgiving to the fourth Thursday of the month. Never again would the country fall prey to the unfortunate fifth Thursday.

The rest is just evolution of the sport.

So the next time you mock a small woman hauling a large box, while wearing pajamas and carrying two wallets, just remember she is doing it for her country.

And buy her a coffee, would you? The good stuff. Not black.

Shallow Thoughts on a Deep Man

IT TOOK HIS HOLINESS THE Dalai Lama three years to respond to the University of Arkansas's invitation to speak on campus, but when he accepted I immediately put it on my calendar. I'd be challenged to find Tibet on a map, but I wasn't going to miss an opportunity to hear one of the world's most influential figures speak. For a year, I knew he was coming, and I fully intended to read up on the Holy Dude, in the hopes of having more appreciation for his talk.

Unfortunately, I got busy with more important things, like filling out enrollment paperwork and cross-referencing my calendar with my to-do list. Ultimately, my only preparation for the big day came from Wikipedia—something about China and reincarnation and Buddhism. It was probably the longest Wikipedia entry I've ever skimmed. It was possible I would not fully benefit from the deep and meaningful words offered by His Holiness. I decided this was for the best. I would experience the historic speech without expectations.

That sounded Zen-ish.

Who Peed on My Yoga Mat?

"I'm in the spirit, right?" I asked my companions as we walked across the University of Arkansas campus.

"Yes, release yourself from the attachment to permanence," one of them said.

"That's easy to say when you've been reincarnated fourteen times."

Not exactly devotees, the three of us, but seekers of insight nonetheless. Ignorant though we were, all of us hoped for a bit of inspiration, a moment of clarity, a breadcrumb of truth with a capital T, while in the presence of the Great Man. We made it through the sub-TSA quality State Department security and found our seats in Bud Walton arena, which must have undergone an aromatherapy intervention. I smelled something distinctly sweet and un-basketball-like.

After only minor ado and pageantry, the Dalai Lama appeared in a bundle of red robes. He wore a visor, presumably to shield his eyes from the bright lights. At the risk of bringing on whatever is the Buddhist form of getting struck by lightning, I have to say the HHDL looked rather like a cuddly poppy-red frog. As part of a panel discussing non-violence as a strategy for peace, he stood out by using far fewer words than anyone else on the panel. Humble in posture, but commanding respect, especially when quieting a group of chanters who seemed to be praying—or possibly protesting. Sometimes it's hard to tell the difference.

Despite the spectacular lighting and the theatrical draping, the Dalai Lama was surprisingly mellow. He was at once wholly authoritative and wholly humble. He was neither showy nor arrogant. He wasn't preachy, but encouraged us to practice compassion and tolerance.

Practice.

Even in the presence of the spiritual leader we tweeted, the most notable update spoofed the utter calmness of the event.

> *@Ozarkbahner — Dalai Lama lowering from arena rafters on stage wire, crowd ERUPTS as opening hook from "Panama" plays! #HHDL #1984*

It takes a special talent to see the correlation between His Holiness and David Lee Roth. I like to think HHDL giggled later at the Van Halen reference, while reviewing his Twitter stream aboard his Holiness jet.

His Holiness was not spectacular. He was smart and funny and utterly charming. Sure, it was tough to make out each and every word, which only made the rest of us shudder when some woman at the top of the arena screamed "Louder!"

Only in Arkansas.

I cringed. But the 14th Dalai Lama was unfazed. He checked his mic and then said, completely without evidence of irritation or drama, "I think the sound is sufficient." All while sitting crossed legged on a couch, and scratching himself as needed. We could use more leaders like this, spiritual or otherwise.

Who Peed on My Yoga Mat?

I like to think our discussion afterwards was a bit elevated by all the holiness, that the message of compassion and connection would last longer than the ride home. We shall see. One thing's sure, I'll never hear Van Halen the same way again.

Bloggers, Beds, and New BFFs

I HAD HEARD THAT BLOGGERS who hadn't actually met in real life often shared rooms at blogging conferences. I read their posts about meeting for the first time offline and lurked among their tweets arranging the aforementioned meet-ups thinking, are those bitches crazy? A few years ago I had trouble spending a weekend in a tiny space with a dear friend. Because, hello? Where are you supposed to go to the bathroom? That is marital-level intimacy, right there. However, I had been on a few girl trips since then. I'd learned to corral my cosmetics and leverage public spaces.

Sadly, I had no BFFs to accompany me to the blogging conference. I thought I might have a good prospect, a blogger I felt I knew, not only because we had chatted a bit, but we had also actually spoken to one another on the phone. I wrote to ask if she was going to the conference, if she needed a roommate, if she "did that sort of thing." Of course I pre-empted her refusal, told her I completely understood if she wasn't interested in sleeping next to a stranger.

"I'm sort of weird about that," she wrote back. "I don't like to share rooms with people I don't already know."

"Oh, I know!" I wrote back. This was followed by too many words about how, again, I completely understood and I wouldn't want to share a room with some crazy bitch like me either! Besides I probably wasn't even going, and hey, did you catch *60 Minutes* last week?

When the time to register got closer I still didn't have a roommate. I wanted to go, but a room to myself would put me over budget. I tweeted something stupid like, "Anyone need a roommate?" and felt the blood leave my body when someone actually responded in the affirmative. Not only did she have a spot available, she would love to have me! Well, now, that doesn't sound crazy at all. I am a damn good roommate, after all. She probably discerned that from my clever tweets and witty Facebook updates.

I knew this woman. She had showed up at my Thursday afternoon parenting chat on Twitter at least five times. By my calculations we must have exchanged at least 2,800 characters. That's like an entire page of text, 12-point font, single-spaced. On the internet that's practically second cousins. I knew things about her that I didn't even know about my own mother, like how she preferred the winky ;) to the straight up smiley :). And how she commented after the RT instead of before it. Plus, she always HA!'d my jokes. How bad could she be?

"Okay!" I DM'd back. "Are you sure?"

"Yes! My roommate will love it."

Roommate? She already had a roommate?

"I don't want to impose," I wrote. "Are there enough beds?"

"Oh, sure, there's a pullout," she wrote back. "It'll be great!"

The next day I found out the existing roommate was someone I also knew. Well, again, I didn't *know* her, but we both freelanced for the same company and had exchanged at least a dozen emails. We were practically sorority sisters. Many excited messages, status updates, and tweets followed in the weeks leading up to the trip. A week before the conference I wrote to my roomies asking the one who had made the reservation to confirm with the hotel that we would have a pull out sofa, or that we could reserve a cot.

"Of course! No problem."

My roommates arrived a day ahead of me. When I arrived they were at a party. Inside the room were dozens of hangers of clothes, at least ten pair of shoes, a double-stocked bathroom, more power cords than the Apple Store, seven or eight swag bags, and two beds.

No pullout.

No cot.

I called the front desk. Wouldn't you know it, no extras. With more than three thousand bloggers bunking up summer camp style. Go figure.

I texted my roommates:

"Don't fight too hard over who gets to sleep with me."

The one who had reserved the room said it would all work out. However, even if the hotel miraculously produced a rollaway, I couldn't see how we'd fit it in the room. No matter. I had dinner plans, which turned into drink plans, which turned into meeting a zillion people at the bar plans. And I still hadn't met the two women I'd be fighting for shower time over the next two days.

Awkward.

When my roommates texted they were back from the party I asked if they minded if I came in late. Bed or no, I wasn't wasting one moment of this trip. Even if I didn't know exactly where I was sleeping.

"No worries," she wrote. "I'm turning in. Running in the morning. Just come on in and crash." Oh, good, she was running too. We'd laugh about this in the morning, while getting ready to run in the conference 5k together.

Two hours later I swiped my card and made my way by the light of my phone over the shoes and swag to my pajamas, cleanser and toothbrush. I set my alarm for 5:30 for the 6:00 run. No way was I going to miss the chance to run the San Diego waterfront. I left the bathroom to find my place to sleep. I had hoped since the girls knew each other, they might have bunked in together and left me a bed of my own. Oh, my delusional optimism.

I shone my blue-white screen light toward each bed, picked the bed that seemed to have the most room, and crawled in. With... someone. Awkward indeed, but there I lay for hours, not sleeping, not moving. It was ridiculous. I know I must have fallen asleep, because my alarm woke me. I raced to shut it off and got back into bed. No one else was getting up. Why weren't they getting up? Weren't they running? I really wanted to run. But, no, I'd skip it. Because the only thing weirder than sleeping with someone you never met would be getting up and leaving, still without meeting her. And I still had no idea who I was sleeping next to because the blackout blinds were drawn.

That was too much. Even for me. Even for BlogHer.

I heard another alarm go off. They were getting up after all!

Not really.

One of them—again, no idea which one—got up and turned off the alarm. Okay, I told myself, just lie here a minute and they'll get up and we'll all go run and it'll be fine.

Or not.

I lay there for a few more minutes. I really, really, really wanted to run. And it wasn't like I was getting any more rest lying next to this stranger. Not to mention I'm sure they'd already made their judgments about me when I chose my new bar friends over online BFFs the night before. Screw it. I got up, got dressed, brushed my teeth, and left.

Ten minutes later I learned the race didn't start at 6:00, but 6:30. Of course. In the pink morning light, I confessed my sleeping arrangements to the first blogger I met. I had to process it, to make some sense of this farce, to somehow get my bearings by expressing the utter absurdity of it all to another human being. But I couldn't, because at every plot point she kept interrupting.

"Me, too!"

"Seriously? You planned to room with people you didn't know?"

"Uh, huh!"

"And then you didn't even meet them before you crawled into bed with one and may or may not have molested her in your sleep?"

"Yep!"

"And then you laced up without so much as a hot morning beverage together out of the bathroom coffee maker?"

"Sure did!"

Well, hello, brand new BFF!

Crazy though I may have been, I was not alone in my insanity. A small comfort, but an important one.

I finally met my roommate a few minutes later. I spotted her—I thought—a few paces ahead while we were running in opposite directions along the course.

"Christie?"

She nodded.

"It's me, Lela!"

"Uh-huh." She barely slowed her pace.

"Hey," I called over my shoulder as I switched to a backwards jog. "Was that you I was sleeping with last night, or Kelly?"

"That was me." Tentative smile.

"Cool!" Big smile, thumbs up. "See you in a bit!"

Later, at a party, I found the blogger who had thwarted my initial advances and told her the story.

"Wow," she said. "You're brave."

"Really? You think? Brave? Not Crazy?"

She gave me that smile one uses when they're not sure the person they're dealing with is on the appropriate medication. "Well, brave because it worked out. If it hadn't, then

I'd be calling you a crazy bitch."
Now that's a friend.
I wonder if she wants to room with me next year.

Of Underwear and Validation

I LEARNED SOMETHING IMPORTANT at Victoria's Secret, and I'm not talking about how to wear a thong. Over a sale bin full of panties and bras, I learned that I had readers. That day at the mall, seeking renewed confidence in underwear, I found purpose instead. Picking through the segregated display of nylon and lace, I looked up to see a pretty blonde mom from my kids' school. I smiled, said hi. We didn't know each other, not really, but she had read something I had written.

And she liked it.

"I think you found your calling," she said.

My worlds collided. In my outside life I compared bunches of kale, tried to identify the smell in the garage, and considered the merits of boy cut versus low-rise briefs. I spent my other life quietly inside my head, scrawling thoughts into spiral notebooks, and tapping them into reality at the keyboard. As these two lives converged, time paused and before me appeared an angel.

Or a Romanian model in a feather bra.

Either way, we had a moment—the mall me, the writer me, and this glorious reader. Was this a sign? Could it be possible that I wasn't actually wasting my time with my scribbling? This woman was only one, but she was one. To me she proved that someone, somewhere, for some ungodly reason derived enjoyment from the utterly narcissistic endeavor that stole time away from real life pursuits, like cleaning the blinds and replacing my underwear.

I had been posting essays on a website that gave me space for a monthly column I called *After the Bubbly*. I had wondered on many occasions if the unpaid gig would get me anything—other than the right to say, "I'm busy now. I'm on deadline." Nothing like an imaginary deadline to validate the writer's soul. Every month I wrote something of my very own. This was 2007, before Facebook became the second home of my friends and peers. I sent emails with links to each newly published essay to a few dozen people I knew. A handful of friends passed these links along to others. It wasn't quite viral, but it was a start. My writing was out there and I assumed some people read it. But I didn't know for sure.

Until now.

This woman, right here at the underwear sale, had read my words.

And, again, this is important: She liked them.

I thanked her and continued to shop, pretending I still needed new underwear to lift my mood. I suddenly knew that all I needed was a reader, a real one—not my neighbor or my best friend or the people in my cat-loving writing group—someone with no vested interest in my ego or my happiness, to witness my experience and validate the efforts I had taken to share it.

Until that moment I didn't know I had readers; I didn't know I needed them.

"I can really tell how much you love your kids," she said. "It really comes through."

I played this over and over in my mind. She got it. She understood me. More importantly, even though I didn't realize it as I wrote the essay, I understood her. By extension, I understood others like her, like me. We writers can be a self-absorbed lot, but we become useful to others when we articulate what they think and feel and feed it back to them with more meaning, more thrill, or more humor than the original offered. No one needs my writing. But they might want it, if I convince them they do. That moment among the delicates helped me to believe that my writing had value for others.

Here, read this. Relax a minute. Smile. Smirk. Laugh—at yourself and this silly wonderful life.

I bought some miracle undergarments that day—stretch lace bikini briefs and a push up bra, because no matter how significant, affirmation lifts only your psyche.

Then I went home to write.

Life on the Cul-de-Sac

The Road to Hell is Covered
in Minivans

I DON'T ACTUALLY DRIVE A MINIVAN, but I know a lot of people who do. So when a single, child-free friend rolled up into my driveway in a smokin' hot gold Odyssey to pick me up for a girls evening out, I didn't judge.

"This thing is so ugly," she said. "And it's hard to drive. Why do people drive these things?"

The unsaid You, as in, "You People," hung heavy in the air. You People, of the 2.5 children. You People with the golf clubs and strollers. You People of Suburban Hell.

When I asked where her car was, I got a long story about a former colleague and a company car and her accommodating driveway. Bottom line: She'd started driving the van just before Thanksgiving because she had to take some things to her parents' house out of state.

"I had stuff to haul."

"That is exactly why Us People drive minivans," I told

her. "We're transporting cargo, too. Ours is live. And snot-laced."

"Well, they're hideous and impossible to park," she said, pulling into an average-sized parking spot.

"So, when did you come home from this stuff-hauling journey?"

"Last week."

"And you're still driving the van?"

She gestured toward the back. "I haven't had a chance to clean it out."

I blame the baby boomers. Today's symbol of domesticity has its roots in the that vehicle so popular with the psyche-delic generation: The Volkswagon van—perfect for taking beaded macramé crafts to the fair or road-tripping to muddy music fests. By 1968 the VW van had all the trademarks of its less groovy descendant, including the sliding side door. Cut to the 80s, when all those love children started trans-porting children of their own and voilà, rise of the minivan.

It's a short trip from groovy to practical to pathetic.

Therein lies the danger of buying, or even borrowing, a minivan. You might have the best intentions, but we know where that road leads. Maybe you only plan to use the eyesore vehicle for a short time—until the kids are out of strollers, or done with soccer, or until you can weasel your way out of that godforsaken carpool. But life happens. Shin guards ac-cumulate, yoga mats and notebooks from the Junior League multiply. French fries solidify under the seats and a school of goldfish crumbs take up residence in the way-way back.

This was already happening to my friend. She may not

have had the trappings of family, but the van had cursed her nonetheless. Piling up in the back were clothes headed for the donation bin, a printer, and two pair of shoes purchased during a hormonal imbalance and waiting to be returned. And there was plenty of room for it all. Unknowingly, she had joined the tribe of You People. Like the rest of them, she'd rather be driving something else, but first she'd have to clean out the van.

And possibly rent a storage unit.

Until then I'm hoping she'll agree to take my place in the carpool rotation.

Go For a Walk?

FIVE BLOCKS FROM HOME, my new puppy stopped mid trot and crapped right on the sidewalk. I imagined home-owners peeking out through their blinds while cursing me to their well-behaved, box-trained cats. This sidewalk incident was a first. Libby had a backyard routine. I liked that routine. It involved my kids picking up poop at home instead of me picking up poop in a neighboring 'hood. So, staring down a dog deuce in the middle of the sidewalk, I did what any rational woman would do. I kicked the poo onto the nicely manicured lawn of the adjacent yard.

I felt awful. Because—pardon the pun—that's a shitty thing to do. However, because I was too far from home to go all the way back, I resigned myself to the guilt and carried on, making some fake pact with myself about how I would make up for this indiscretion. Perhaps I could pick up some other dog's abandoned turds on my next walk. Just as I'd accepted my crime, a woman emerged onto a nearby driveway, attempting to load two preschoolers and enough gear to hike the Appalachian Trail into a minivan.

"Do you happen to have a plastic trash bag?" I asked. "A Walmart bag?"

I explained while gesturing to my super cute doggie. "She made a mess back there on the sidewalk and I didn't bring anything."

The woman obliged, like I knew she would. In these parts, everyone's got a Walmart bag. And who wouldn't want to help me keep the neighborhood clean? I waited while her three-year-old fetched a sack and then thanked them more than was necessary. On the way back to the scene of the crime, I congratulated myself. The imaginary judgmental home-owner probably didn't even exist. I could have gotten away with my irresponsible feces management. But I had done the right thing. I felt like a quite a decent person as I walked down the street with a bag full of warm poop dangling from my dog's leash.

Libby and I enjoyed our walk, me noticing flowers and her tracking the airborne evidence of squirrels and rabbits. An older man passed us, smiling and nodding at my sweet puppy. All was well in our world until we passed a stretch where big cars drove fast. Libby got scared. She spooked again when we had to pass a big barking alpha dog. But my new best friend stuck close and I took pride in my ability to instill in her a trust that all things scary could not harm her when she walked beside me. We made our way to the end of the long loop and were heading in the direction of home when a truck frightened my dog so badly that she literally lost it.

Right there on the sidewalk.

Again.

But not so tidy this time. The fear-motivated bowel moves quickly. The plastic bag couldn't help me here so I scraped the sole of my tennis shoe across the messy sidewalk, trying to clean up after us, while simultaneously trying to keep my panicky dog from stepping in it. I was unsuccessful in both efforts.

Finally, I surrendered.

Walking away from the crap-covered sidewalk I consoled myself with the fact that the next good rain would surely take care of things. A few blocks from home I encountered the friendly older gentleman again.

"That sure is a nice-looking dog," he said. I smiled, sweet as I could, and considered warning him about what he was walking into.

Nah. Let him like us for five more minutes before his illusions are covered in dog fear.

Next time we walk, I'll bring two bags and a spray bottle.

Or I'll just leave Libby in the back yard.

Cotillion: Season of the Mom

IT IS NOT ENOUGH THAT WE SEND them to cotillion, where they learn the art of waiting for a boy to march by, who by the luck of the line will become their dance partner for the evening. It is not enough that they dress up in clothing they likely will never wear again in order to look the part— God knows the white gloves and "hosiery" go beyond any reasonable expectation. It is not enough that we present them at a ball at the end of the season, where they show off their newly acquired skill at dancing with a member of the opposite sex without spraying themselves with an imaginary can of Cootie Remover. All this we do so that they might become well-mannered ladies and gentlemen.

But apparently we have to control their entire social life while we're at it.

The first year my son was enrolled in cotillion I thought the whole thing rather silly, but you never know when dancing in a line may prove to be a social advantage. The second year I came around. This was when the boys started following the girls to the ice cream shop or the laser tag center or the mall food court after the dance. These "after parties" were the real reason the boys agreed to don sport jackets and ties.

We are now in Year Three for the boy, and the first year for my daughter. She acts like she doesn't like it, but I know a part of her likes the excuse to get dressed up, in spite of the pantyhose. The day of the first dance, she and her friends texted pictures of themselves in various dresses, headbands, and earrings while I finalized a complicated drop off and pickup schedule, carefully balancing the duties so that no moms were unfairly burdened with the pickup-and-take-out-after shifts. The children may act like they are the ones suffering through cotillion, but it's the parents who sacrifice six Saturday nights to be personal chauffeurs and cash machines.

Because I made the schedule, I gave myself the dreaded task of after-party duty on the first night. Throughout the afternoon I received calls, texts, and emails from moms asking me where we were going.

"I don't know," I replied. "Wherever the girls decide to go."

"Didn't you get the email?"

Oh, yes, I had gotten the email—the one laying out a schedule of where all the 6th grade girls from my daughter's school would be going after each cotillion class. But this was optional, yes? Especially since the first night had them slotted for evening festivities at a nice chain restaurant frequented by the over-70 set. Not the best choice for a passel of 'tween girls who had just spent an hour touching boys.

I learned better when I picked them up.

"Where do you want to go?"

"Mimi's!" they screamed.

"Really?"

"We have to go to Mimi's," one girl said.

"You don't have to," I told them. "We can go wherever you want."

"My mom said we have to go to Mimi's," said one girl.

"Yeah, my mom's meeting us there," said another.

Seriously? A mom whose child had a perfectly good ride home was subjecting herself to the pain of "after cotillion"? And how did I miss this convening of the mothers in the day's many messages, phone calls, and Facebook status updates? And why couldn't we just go get frozen yogurt?

I turned up the radio, let the girls shriek, and got over myself. This was about the girls and I was happy to follow their consensus. At the restaurant, we filled the lobby with squeals and taffeta. Luckily, the Mother-in-Charge had reserved the back room for twenty-five of us. I sat with some women I knew, but not well. We discussed pediatrician appointments and the dilemma of finding the right dress, and the safety merits of making kids sit in the backseat. Because we had been assigned a single waitress, we waited half an hour to get our drinks, and twice as long to get our bills. In between the girls were hushed and corralled unnaturally. I marshaled all my will to keep from saying, "It's better when we take them to TCBY."

I failed.

I didn't want to hurt Mother-in-Charge's feelings. She

was only trying to make things nice, and had gone to great lengths to include everyone. And yet, I also wanted to punch her in the face. Maybe I'm the one who needs cotillion.

I found out later (and would have learned sooner if I'd read the entire email thread) that this first night out after cotillion was supposed to be mother-daughter night. (Never mind that there were two boys dragged into the mix.) Here's my issue: Why does everything have to be special? And when everything is special, doesn't that mean nothing is special? There are exceptional Valentine's parties and magical Cookies with Santa, enchanting Father-Daughter dances and extraordinary Field Days. When do these children of fortune ever get a break from all this specialness and just get to be kids? And how much of the desire to create all of these outstanding memories is Mommy Ego and how much of it is truly for the kids?

I'd like to believe that these mothers have better things to do on a Saturday night than intrude upon their daughters' social lives. In fact, I could tell by their demeanor exactly which moms would have preferred to be anywhere else, or at least somewhere that did not involve artificially engaging with other moms only because our daughters went to school together. How was this a special Mother-Daughter time? Our daughters wanted nothing to do with us on a Saturday night. Even at eleven they have more appealing alternatives. And that's okay.

I take my Mother-Daughter bonding where I can get it. Surreptitiously stealing moments that she doesn't realize are important—when I tuck her into bed, riding side by side in the front seat of the car, chopping cucumbers for the salad and letting her take as many as she likes. I know I'm too hard on the other type of mothers—the ones I find overzealous in their desire to guide every waking moment of their children's existence. Maybe it's just post 9/11 hover-parenting, or a southern charm I'll never possess.

Or maybe one of us needs to back off and get over herself.

I'm just not sure it's me.

Lessons from the Elk River

I LIVE IN THE OZARKS, where people are fond of getting in a canoe or a raft and floating down a river. In the name of adventure and anthropological curiosity, I have joined them. During our first float trip we witnessed the fishing technique called noodling where a fisherman sticks his hand into a pile of rocks on the riverbank hoping to grab a fish. Sometimes the fishermen get bitten, but usually they just fall over and shout the kind of obscenities you can only learn if you grow up among hill people. We also watched a woman nearly topple a boat while lunging over the side of her canoe, trying to rescue a handle of whiskey from the rapids. It's fun for the kids.

If you think I got my fill of culture on the first trip, you just don't get me. Floating is the thing to do. It's BIG. Also, we didn't have any other plans for the Fourth of July and it sounded more fun than watching our neighbor fertilize the grass. We met some friends at a canoe rental place on the Elk River, known for its varying water levels and rednecky goodness. Because I have been trained by my good Southern girlfriends to "dress to the invitation," I donned cutoff Levi shorts and a hat I like to call Dixie Chick chic. I packed a cooler and headed out with my family for a nine-mile ride. Very little of our time on the river could be described as floating.

A trip down the Elk may be considered the peak of bliss in these parts, but where I come from we don't even have canoes. It's just you, your Pabst Blue Ribbon, and an inner tube lifted from a nearby junkyard. Still, there are lessons here. The things I learned on the Elk River are nothing new, but ancient wisdom in life's classroom.

Never stand up in a canoe. Just don't.

Climbing into a boat is easier on shore than mid-stream. Almost always.

In related good news, bleeding into a river does not attract sharks.

Believe the guy who says, "By noon, this will burn off."

Not everyone needs SPF 600. But I do.

City girls aren't the only ones who seem to find out early how to open doors with just a smile—or a lift of a beaded crop top. Parents should prepare an answer to the question, "Why is that man wearing all those necklaces?"

You never know who will push you out of a low spot, and sometimes people surprise you.

For maximum relaxation, never separate competitive siblings. Put them in the same boat and "race" against them. They will always win. And so will you.

There is no such thing as too much river beer.

Tube tops and string bikinis should have an expiration date. The actual date varies, depending on just how hard a life you've lived, but pick a milestone birthday—21, 30, 40, 65—and stick with it.

One sandwich is never enough.

The last quarter-mile is always the hardest.

Always bring your phone. And duct tape. No exceptions.

"We should do this more often" actually means "We should do this again in a few years."

And again, in case you forgot already—never stand up in a canoe.

Drive-In Movie, Saturday Night

IT WAS OVER NINETY DEGREES when we packed the truck and headed to the drive-in. Admission is $12 a carload, which covers a spot on the gravel and access to the audio. The movies are mostly for kids, but we're not here for filmmaking. We come for ambiance and memories. For us, the drive-in is an annual thing, a pilgrimage if you will. Where else can you sit under the stars, watch those snack bar commercials from the 60s, and eat yesterdays' popcorn? If you're lucky you get a storm in the distance or see shooting stars.

Then there's the people watching. At $12 a carload, anyone with enough cousins to pitch in a dollar can pile into 1982 Winstar and descend upon the spot next to you. The drive-in is my favorite place to observe pregnant teenagers and their tattooed, pajama-wearing mothers dragging toddlers with one hand while holding cigarettes in the other.

Twelve-ounce drinks are $3.50, so I always bring a cooler, but last time we went my daughter brought a friend who didn't like my selection. I handed the kids ten dollars and sent them to the snack bar. It wasn't truly dark yet, and it's not like the shirtless guy with the nipple rings is going to make his move before dusk, right? They came back with a Styrofoam cup and a handful of money.

"Why do you have all that money?"

"We were like fifteen cents short so some lady paid for it."

"Some lady paid for what?"

My daughter held out her cup of Sprite. "This."

"Why didn't you just come back and get more money?"

She started nodding and rolling her eyes. "I know, right? That's what we were going to do. We were all like, 'We're going to get some more money' and then this lady was like, 'Don't worry about it, Hon. I'll get it.'"

I looked at their feet. Both were still wearing shoes, flip-flops at least. They'd bathed in the last 24 hours, and were wearing clothes without rips or stains (somewhat unusual) so I figured fine, let it go. Someone bought your poor disadvantaged children a soda. Be grateful and move on.

After the first movie I took my daughter and her friend to the bathroom. You have to be quick. In between movies a line forms fast and you don't want your 11-year-old subjected to talk of bail and Chlamydia any longer than necessary. Plus that nipple ring guy parks just outside the ladies room. We maneuvered through the local color and headed back to the truck, where there was much resettling of lawn chairs and sleeping bags before the second show. The audio doesn't come through those cool pole-mounted speakers anymore. You have to tune in to the designated radio frequency. Some families left, others fired up their engines to make sure the battery didn't die. Others kicked on the A/C. When the second movie started the car next to us was still idling. Made it tough to hear, but surely they'd cut the engine soon.

Nope.

Forty-five excruciating minutes later, our rude neighbors were still enjoying the cool breeze coming off the dash as I struggled to make out the plot of Rio, the Horny Parrot. I could have said something. I got up several times, stood next to their car, tried to catch a glimpse of the kind of people who would blatantly flout drive-in etiquette. Not to mention waste gas and run the risk of overheating their engine. Who does that?

I considered alerting security at the snack bar, but did this really merit a higher authority? Besides, the drive-in is a family business and I knew they were probably busy making popcorn for next week. And while I was worried we all might die from carbon monoxide poisoning—it's not like that summer air was moving—the kids weren't bothered at all, and this was supposed to be about them. And who knows who you're dealing with out there in the heated night? Nothing ruins a evening at the drive-in like a knife fight in row four.

So I focused on the inordinate number of shooting stars, which turned out to be moths lighting up in the projected light. I didn't say anything to the horrible wastes of humanity in the next car. I didn't understand the movie. I got pissy with my husband, which prompted him also to stand up and do nothing besides sit back down and proclaim, "Jackasses are going to leave their engine running the whole movie."

It's not like there's a rule against it. It's not like they're using their cell phones in a theater. But once it was over I showed them. Gave them a big sarcastic thumbs up.

They'll think twice next time. I'm sure of it.

As for us, we've already marked the calendar for next year's outing at the drive-in, with a note: Leave after the first movie.

The Real Reason I was Blacklisted from the PTA

I DIDN'T HAVE TIME TO PICK A FIGHT. Why bother? I'd put up with the brown recluse spider cover-up and the school nurse's blind eye to lice. I had ignored the cancellation of Spanish classes and the denial of chess club because there were no classrooms available after school. Never mind there was plenty of room in the hallway for the Gideons to distribute their version of the Bible. I hadn't complained that the powers of education were so concerned about my child's moral development that they teach abstinence instead of safe sex. Besides, those were district decisions.

This was different. It was PTA. And nobody messes with the PTA. These are the women who determine which kids get the best teachers, who gets invited to the extra special parties, and who gets the lead in the school play.

Why start with the fundraiser?

What was I thinking?

Didn't I realize this particular fundraiser would mean a

record-setting year for the elementary school carnival?

Wasn't I going to get on board, silence my concerns like every other rational mother had done?

Did I know who I was dealing with?

Didn't I know my place?

Images of replica handguns and assault rifles—forty percent off retail—in all their full color glory, filled my MacBook screen. Are you kidding me? On another day I might have ended it with a disgusted click to delete the email, but that message, those images, in that moment, put me over the edge.

I quickly learned that the Airsoft guns donated for sale at our fundraiser simulate the experience of shooting a real gun through a carefully crafted combination of appearance, weight, and kickback. Many look so believable that police have been unable to distinguish them from the real thing. Officers have drawn weapons on children brandishing these asinine toys. But here in the bubble of privilege and affluence, it's all about the money. I wondered what a mother in some inner city school would think of us encouraging our sheltered kids to playact gang violence. As one of the most demographically advantaged schools in the district, our carnival brings in thousands every year. But, apparently, we need more. The bottom line, according to the auction committee chair, was five thousand dollars.

Several years ago the Junior League here was offered ten thousand dollars from *Hooters*. We work against domestic violence and part of that work includes building up girls' self-esteem. Maybe the average Hooter Girl is well-adjusted and not the least exploited by those tiny t-shirts and short shorts, but accepting the gift would have sent the wrong message so we declined—on principle.

Five grand. Guns. Little kids.

Columbine and Virginia Tech are reason enough for a school to avoid association with guns—real or otherwise. And you have to be eighteen years old to buy one of these. They are prohibited on school property—just like real guns, which is weird, because that's where the fundraiser was supposed to be.

I called the PTA President to voice my concern that this was not an appropriate partnership.

"It's just a donation," she said, like we were talking about bottled water for Field Day.

I talked to the room mom who sent the flyer advertising the faux firearms. She didn't agree with the fundraiser, either. She said it made her a little sick, but she didn't speak up. Still, her opposition, spoken or not, was the support I needed to continue the battle.

I called the auction committee chair, asking her to cede to her better judgment.

"Oh I knew it would be controversial," she said.

That's why she made sure no policies were violated and administered the fundraiser tastefully and discreetly.

"If you notice, I didn't even use the word gun in the flyer." She knew the project was wrong, but justified it as a win-win. "Look," she said, "parents are going to buy these for their kids anyway."

I thought of AshleyMadison.com, the dating website for

infidelity, and their tagline: *Life is short, have an affair.* People cheat anyway; why not profit from it? By that reasoning we should have sold cigarettes and homicidal video games. Anything for new playground equipment!

The auction chair also liked the idea of having something so convincing in the house. You know, for protection, in case the guys with the real guns show up.

I spoke to the principal, who shared my views, but unfortunately not my outrage. She had turned the guns away at the school door, but this wasn't any of her concern. The fundraiser was PTA business. It didn't matter that a student could be expelled for bringing an Airsoft gun to school, might be suspended for pointing a finger or holding a banana the wrong way. She wasn't compelled to take a stand.

After I left a message with the superintendent, I sent an email to everyone I know at school, urging them to respectfully request putting a stop to the fundraiser. There was plenty of silence, but I only got two emails in dissent. Their counter to my arguments went like this:

"If you have strong feelings, you should have been on the committee."

Translation: If you're not in charge, shut up.

People tell you your opinion doesn't count hoping you'll believe it and back off. If you do, they've won without having to defend their position. I am a member of the PTA. They were conducting business in my name. Whether or not I ever paint a bulletin board, collate a stack of flyers, or chair a committee, I have a say. God forbid you rouse the Mean Girls living inside those PTA moms. One particularly offended woman said that no one at school would ever speak to me again. It sounded familiar, like something I heard the time I wouldn't let Jessica Martin copy off my ninth grade science test.

Someone actually said to me, "You know they're not real guns, right?" As if I were either completely uninformed, un-intelligent, or so easily influenced that I would come to my senses once I realized they were just harmless toys. But they aren't. They are stupid imitation guns that dull the sense of danger, and the repercussions, of firing real weapons.

Just before the carnival, the PTA and the school delivered a small victory. The Airsoft guns were banned from school grounds and the company would not be allowed to set up a table at the carnival. However, preorders would be honored; it was only fair. So the guns were still sold.

Quietly.

Discreetly.

Not really a win, but I believe my small revolt mattered. Next time one more person will speak out—the time after that, another. They will learn, as I have, that confrontation is not so bad, just uncomfortable and time consuming.

And maybe next year, I'll serve on the auction commit-tee.

Marital Bliss

Showered in Miscommunication

Experts insist that the key to a long and happy relationship is communication. Titles of almost all the best-selling books about marriage include the words language, talking, or conversation. Having spent two decades with the same man, I assure you, communication is overrated. Or at least, misunderstood. Sex—now that's a worthy goal. Nothing like a little physical communication to cure what ails you. Hotel sex? Even better.

To this end my husband and I packed an overnight bag and tossed a twenty at the kids on our way to Eureka Springs for some much needed time away. We had reservations in a lovely haunted hotel, complete with tall ceilings, warped windows, and hundred-year-old furniture. After we'd settled in and opened the same Riesling we drank on our honeymoon, I showered and started to get ready for our big night out. (Where big night out = eating pasta on a deserted balcony at the only restaurant that stays open past eight o'clock.)

I was at the sink setting up the hair infrastructure when

John started opening the drawers to the dresser. He pulled out a penguin made of terry cloth and that soft and scrubby net material, something you'd find overflowing from a basket at *Bath and Body Works* next to the Exotic Coconut Body Butter.

"It's a loofah." He turned it around in his hands, examining how it was constructed.

"It's not a loofah," I corrected, "and I can't believe you're touching it."

He looked at me. He looked at the penguin. He didn't say anything.

"Seriously," I said. "Put it down."

He put the penguin back in the drawer and closed it slowly, methodically.

"What is your deal?"

"What is MY deal? You're the one molesting someone else's scrubby." I shook my head and reached for more wine. "That's disgusting."

What he wanted to say: *Get over it, you freakish germaphobe.*

What he actually said: "Yeah, I guess you're right."

I applied a second coat of mascara as my husband came up from behind me and put his hands around my waist.

"Gross! Wash your hands."

"Why?" He really didn't get it.

And this, I guess, is where that communication thing comes in. It's just that there are certain truths one assumes that another knows. Did I really have to spell it out? I did.

"I don't want someone else's ass germs on me."

Confusion washed across his face. "Oh, come on." He shook his head. "The face thingy?"

I stopped applying blush. Surely this wasn't happening. Absolutely this has had to come up in the last twenty years. I tread carefully. "That's not what it's for."

The confusion on John's face was replaced by an ugly realization.

"So... that thing hanging in our shower—that fluffy thing? You use it... on your—"

"Ass crack."

"No! You're lying!"

And then it was my turn to have an epiphany. "You don't really use it on your face, do you?"

He sighed, heavily, sat down on the ancient sofa, and emptied the bottle into his glass. He remained in denial. It took several minutes to convince him that I wasn't just messing with him. "It's scrubby and soft," I told him. "That's what it's for. It's an ass scrubber."

Communication, it's a beautiful thing.

He shook his head in disbelief, staring out the window, saying more to himself than to me, "I specifically don't use that thing on my ass because I know it's for your face."

I conjured my gentlest tone of voice. "That's funny, Babe. Because I specifically don't use that thing on my face because I know it's for your ass."

Working the Goatee

THE MADRID AIRPORT LAUNCHES us into a family mutiny over where to eat breakfast. We end up eating twice. Croissants the first time and cheeseburgers on round two, all because my husband won't listen to me and my carefully calculated travel day meal plan.

John is in a perpetual state of panic. Twenty-plus hours of running and waiting, only to run again, and wait again. Every airport, every ticket counter, every gate, is reason for extreme anxiety. Perhaps for good reason. With a name like "John Davidson," and a travel history that includes more than one Middle Eastern country, it's no wonder my husband has made The List—not the No-Fly List, more like the "You've Been Randomly Selected for Security Check AGAIN" List. So what if we had to board without him on leg two of the long journey home? It's not like he's not used to it.

At least he looks good.

A white cotton button-down shirt emphasizes his two-week tan. (It only took me fifteen years to convince him to wear the shirts he protested made him look like a "Young Republican.") His hair, too, seems whiter, sparsely threaded with the remaining dark gray. He knows he looks good, but he thinks it's the goatee. In twenty years I have never seen John with any kind of beard, but on the last weekend of our extended holiday he decided to let it grow. Sketchy whiskers. Always a good choice for a para-terror suspect.

It's not all bad, though. While I'm not sure I like the look, I do like the attitude that comes with it. John is acting naughty, devilish even. The image of Satan is usually a variation on Pan, the ancient Greek half-man, half-goat god who loved music, dancing, and sex. And the dude had a goatee. Swap the flute with a pitchfork and you have the ideal ruler of hell. Or nightclubs. Goatees got game, is all I'm saying.

In Spain I had bet John his new image wouldn't last through the morning routine of his first day back in the States. However, here on the ten-hour flight from Madrid to Dallas it's working for him. A flight attendant starts paying special attention after he helps close the overhead bins that are out of her reach. Oh, boy, is she appreciative, maybe because John is separated from his family, across the aisle from the kids and me. Then again, maybe it really is the sexy chin hair that compels our over-50 flight attendant to slip him three bottles of gin.

"You'd better watch out, Mom," my son says. "Dad's going to trade you in."

As if he could afford her insurance premiums.

My daughter is more practical. "She's giving him that

stuff for free?" I nod. "Make sure she doesn't find out he's got a wife." The kids and I devise a plan to score extra Chex Mix and Dr. Pepper.

When I get up to use the restroom, the flight attendant tells me what a nice man my husband is. I agree and listen to her stories of too-tall compartments and rare gentlemen flyers. Later, she brings wine with my dinner. Maybe it's the altitude, or the Chardonnay, but I'm feeling affectionate toward the man who personified impatience and arrogance all day. For just a moment, I see my husband the way the flight attendant sees him—like a handsome goat, who is not above his share of manual labor. For this I'm grateful. Now, if he'd only up his game, we might get moved to first class.

Calendar This

MY HUSBAND'S COMPANY RECENTLY switched from the antiquated Lotus Notes to Google for all their messaging. This was the catalyst for me to finally convert from an equally obsolete paper calendar to an electronic one. My husband and I could finally synchronize our calendars. Never again would we speak in clipped tones about the "surprise" soccer practice or missed dental appointment. And all without persistent verbal reminders from me. Either one of us could create an event and invite the other to it. Finally, a solution for eight out of ten of our marital disputes.

The first thing I did—after filling in the requisite parent-teacher conferences and basketball games—was invite my husband to: Sex, Tuesday, 6:30 am. I received his response right away. He declined. Then the phone rang. However, I was busy scheduling good intentions into all those rectangles, so my husband left a message with our daughter. She handed me the note, written in her childish scrawl:

Dad says that's not funny. He could get fired for that.

This did not bode well for the new system. If I couldn't get my husband to pay attention to such an inviting appointment, what chance did I have with morning carpool?

I've had a thing for calendars since I was a 20-year-old bank teller with my first At-A-Glance. It showed a full month in square-inch boxes, few of which actually had anything written in them. I like calendars so much that I keep them. Deep in the back of my closet are chronological records dating back to 1991. If some future descendant ever wants to reconstruct my life, he or she could plot the highlights: met my husband, graduated college, got married, had a baby, had another baby, etc. through the scribbled evidence of my days. These boxes may someday provide valuable insights about life at the turn of the century. Right there on December 31, 1999 it reads: Y2K Semiahmoo. A party at the end of the world. Except that the plans I had in the weeks following came to pass. The apocalypse did not arrive as promised. Instead, I got a haircut and went to a pre-natal appointment.

I'm a little sad I won't have those physical mementos anymore, but I'm not going back. Much as I love paper, you can't access a 8 ½ x 11 spiral bound calendar from a smart phone. My attachment to seeing the whole month on one page held me back for years. It hurt my back to carry a stone-age calendar around in my bag. I envied friends who whipped out their phones to schedule appointments. Online calendars are the over-committed woman's crack pipe, and I loved mine from my first hit. The high-tech convenience enables—no, encourages—the tendency to over-schedule by making every obligation fit so easily and efficiently among the others.

My husband liked his new calendar too, but the longer we used our new toys, the clearer it became that being on the same electronic page did not help to synchronize our schedules. Immediately after inviting him to sex I added all my trips to his electronic calendar. Together, we reviewed a print copy to identify any potential conflicts or gaps in child-care coverage. With highlighted boxes and multiple email alerts in place, we were golden.

Not so fast, Execu-Mom.

A few months later my husband "just now remembered" a very important trip he had scheduled "a long time ago." With complete disregard for my carefully crafted minute-by-minute timetable, he had planned this trip without consulting his digital calendar or the handy paper backup. When he suddenly recalled this critical trip that could not be rearranged, I remained calm. As did he. My outer peace was an intentional strategy to resist the strong urge to solve the problem for him, after I stabbed him with a highlighter.

His serenity was based in blind faith.

"My parents can come up," he said.

This is his go-to answer for all childcare, home im-provement, and pet sitting needs. Never mind that his parents, with a combined age of 163, maintain a fully loaded bridge and travel schedule of their own, and live five hours away by car. Surely they would drop everything to pack up the fish oil capsules and merlot and race off to babysit the grandkids. I did not ask my husband if he would make actual requests for definite dates, and then record those dates in a systematic way, such as on a calendar. To do so would have displayed a lack of faith in him.

He said he'd take care of it and I trusted him to do so.

A week before our coinciding trips, feeling guilty about missing my daughter's only band concert of the year, I reassured her that her grandparents would be there to watch her.

"They don't get to see you do this kind of thing very often. It's special."

My husband was in earshot.

"Hey, um..." he said, "have you... um.... talked to my mom at all?"

"About what?"

He started to scratch his head, just like his father does when he's frustrated. "Are they coming up next week?"

Oh, the things I did to him in my mind, things right out of a Mexican soap opera.

Which brings us back to sex, and those handy invitations. For all my love of a good planner, and all my lists and matrices, I never thought I'd become someone who put sex on a calendar. Sure, the invitation started as a joke, but seeing the words there on my screen so official and certain in a business-like font has its merits.

If only I can get my husband to accept my invitations.

Of Pots and Wind Chimes

THE BACKYARD HAS BECOME a point of contention in
my marriage. My husband has created this space for himself
that is peaceful and beautiful, and full of stuff. Nothing is
safe from captivity in our backyard. Pots, beds, more pots,
furniture, little metal thingies, more pots, gravel, tables,
weird-looking plants, more pots. As of last summer, we became wind chime people. Soon we will erect a bottle tree
next to the lilac, learn to play the didgeridoo, and make new
friends who come over to burn sage, sip absinthe, and read
our tarot cards. We are this close to going on the road to
follow Phish.

If that man brings home a gnome, it is over.

Now, at the back door, John stands all sweaty and brood-
ing, while I try to cook dinner.

"Can you look at something?"

I muster the kindest tone possible when one's hands
are covered in shitake. "What is it?"

"Just look through the window." He gestures toward the

Magnolia tree. "What do you think?"

He has arranged a white rope around the tree in the shape of a kidney. I know audibly sighing is a bad habit, but I've almost broken myself of eye rolling and a girl's got to cling to something. So I sigh, which is actually the height of restraint because what I want to say is,

For the love of Martha Stewart how many times do I have to beg you to stop adding crap to the backyard?

I'd be happy with a few shrubs and some of those ready-made hanging baskets, but my husband lives for that yard. He has a seemingly infinite capacity to sit Zen-master-like, while I have to pay a yoga instructor $65 an hour to tell me to be still and breathe. I admire his ability to relax. Sometimes.

My stance on the flowerbed issue has been clear for some time. My husband sees additional beds and borders as an extension of his personal Shangri-La; I see them as the never-ending maintenance they are. My husband loves projects. And he loves to sit on the deck and enjoy the results. What he doesn't love is the upkeep. That's my job. He mows and edges and puts in all these fabulous beds, and my job is to weed them. I'm thinking about the new weeds these beds will bring. And, far be it from me to put a price on Backyard Paradise, but it's expensive.

All this is encapsulated within my sigh. Still, I can't pass up a chance to use my words. "Why do we keep having this conversation?"

His body language tenses for battle and he uses a full extension of both arms to point to the potential bed. "Look, I just need to know if you like the shape."

We stare intently at one another, in a standoff until he breaks. "You'd better tell me if it's ugly."

We both know what's at stake. About a month ago—on Father's Day—John had some excess energy and grand plans to transform our backyard into the grounds of a Mediterranean villa. Before I could utter, *let's think this through*, he was gone and back again from Home Depot with a truckload of terra cotta pots and assorted fancy plants. Still, they were far from his inspiration, the vibrant geraniums we'd seen in Spain. I guess they were out of stock. But you know what? It was Father's Day, damn it! If he wanted to go all P. Allen Smith on us who was I to complain? In hindsight, I know I should have spoken up. Instead, I let him enjoy his project. Sure, it seemed a little unconventional to bury clusters of pots in the grass, but he had vision, I figured. Plus, it was Father's Day. And he wanted to include the kids. What a guy.

I should have said something, anything. Especially when my daughter burst into the kitchen pleading, "Mom, you HAVE to do something. It's terrible!"

Instead, like a Very Good Wife, I lied. "Looks good, Babe," I said.

"Really? You think it's okay?" my husband asked. "It'll really pop when—" Here's where he described his next project. I stopped paying attention, using all my cognitive power to block the image of the desecrated lawn before me. Surely, it would look better in the morning, when my blood pressure went down.

Or not.

Imagine you had a lot of pots on your patio, and there

was a really bad storm that blew them all into the yard. Now picture all the plants in those pots are strewn upon the grass around the pots. And envision, if you will, the grass already growing up through the flowers' foliage. That was the abomination outside my window the next morning. I drove around all day from errand to errand fighting anxiety attacks about how to get the pots out of my yard, but I was determined to broach the subject with tact. I would absolutely say the right thing. I planned to do that sandwich technique where you smother criticism in between two true-but-only-mentioned-to-blunt-the-blow statements. I would time the request just right.

When the phone rang, I was ready.

"I'm going to the gym after work," my husband said.

"Great!" Cheerful tone: check. "I have a meeting at the library," I said. So far, so good. Until... I swear it just jumped out of my mouth. "And then after that I'm going to come home and help you get those things out of the yard."

I felt his disappointment. And then, "They're... bad?"

"They're not good."

"Why didn't you tell me?"

"I um... didn't know they were that... um... bad?"

We both knew the truth. John even admitted that he had known how awful they looked in his gut, but wanted someone to tell him so. By the time I got home from the meeting there were three clumps of dirt where the pot disasters had been.

Those mounds are still visible in the lawn, now a few paces to the right of this new idea, lying on the grass like a dead snake. My husband stands in the doorway, waiting for my opinion on his new endeavor while I remove the stems from my portabellas.

"You know how I feel about this," I say.

"Just tell me if it looks good."

Good is relative, I'm thinking. But I don't say it out loud. I say nothing.

"Fine," he said, "But it's either that or just make a circle and put some mulch around it."

Finally, I think he's coming around. Maybe next week we can renegotiate the wind chimes.

Top 10 Things Men Should
Know About Women

TECHNOLOGICALLY ADVANCED AS we've become, communication between the sexes does not seem to be getting
any easier. To the contrary, our plugged in, always on, any-
thing-is-possible age can make us believe we truly are the
center of the universe. That is clearly a delusion, because
everyone knows the real epicenter of all that is good and true
and right is sex—consensual, committed, prolonged and mutually satisfying sex. It just makes everything better. But in
order to get it, we've got to get along. To that end, I offer
some wisdom from the other side. Use it wisely, my testos-
terone-filled friends, so that we all may be happier.

1. Lysol will get you laid.

Some men might be surprised to learn how far a little
elbow grease goes toward making a woman feel appreciated.
In an unscientific poll, women of all ages revealed their
biggest turn-on was a man pushing a vacuum. The scent of

Formula 409 has actually been shown to be an aphrodisiac if the aroma is detected suddenly, as in walking into a freshly cleaned house. Ironically, scientists also found that very same odor activates the anger center in the female brain when it is inhaled for prolonged periods, especially when hunched over a houseful of toilets afflicted with the typical male aim issues. While this phenomenon of cleanliness-is-next-to-sexiness is nearly universal, if your current domestic arrangement requires you to clean on a regular basis, the sensual effects of doing so are somewhat diminished. Not to worry. It's not really about the cleaning at all; it's about taking a dreaded, mundane, thankless job off her to-do list. To make a woman exceedingly happy, simply identify that which she dreads most, that which exhausts precious wine-drinking-girlfriend-bonding-shoe-shopping hours out of her day, and do it for her. Instant appreciation.

2. Asking for directions, also a turn-on.

Stopping in at the convenience store can diffuse a volatile road trip situation, but there are more important times to ask for guidance. I'm talking about sex again. Believe you me, we'd like to find that G-Spot, too. Every. Single. Time. But just as with air conditioner repairs and software upgrades, nothing is as easy as they tell you in the manual. Still, generally speaking, we know more about our bodies than you do, so ask for directions. Many of us are too shy to simply start directing traffic, so to speak. Let us know you are receptive to learning the territory and we'll give you the map. If you still get lost, remember there's an app for that. It takes batteries.

3. We get it that you're visual. Seriously.

While it's true most of us dress primarily to impress other women, we want your attention, too. And most of us aren't going to file suit against you for complimenting our new dress, so long as you don't go all Herman Cain. Enjoy the view, but don't creep us out. There's a fine line between healthy appreciation and stalker eyes. As for the woman you are supposed to be looking at, when you are out with her, try to control your visual urges. And if you pull out a vertebra while checking out a stunning Other Woman, do not expect sympathy. Expect instead for your evening to end watching Conan alone in your boxers while hopped up on Advil. (Even Lysol won't get you out of this one.) That said, we are reasonable. This visual thing is biology, we understand. For the most part we don't hold it against you. We know it takes a lot of discipline to refrain from admiring every low-rise jean and miracle chest that crosses your path. But it's such an important skill. Maybe one of you could develop something to teach it, perhaps a video game where you earn points by ignoring alluring avatars. Especially as we get older, women need to know that your primordial brain is not being dragged off against its will to younger, smoother, plumper sights. Or, at least that your eyes are the only things that stray.

4. Exfoliation is our domain.

We don't want to smell you until we've committed to a skin-on-skin encounter. That goes for the pleasant smells and the unpleasant. Use your judgment with AXE. We want you to be clean, not Jersey Shore-worthy. Also, we really are less visual than you. (Why else would so many of us date men who are old enough to be our fathers?) Forego the metro. It's bad enough that we have to use all that crap. Basic is better. And while we're on the subject of basic presentation, when it comes to the closet, do yourself a favor and learn how to put an outfit together. It's okay to ask our opinion once in a while, or inquire about a dress code for a particular function, but we don't want to dress you every day. (In related news, don't call me Mommy.) This is particularly true when we are trying to get ourselves ready. Asking a woman for help when she is in the last-minute frenzy of hair, makeup, shoes, and accessory coordination is likely to result in your getting intimate with the business end of a hairbrush.

5. Funny is sexy.

Owen Wilson couldn't get lucky in a women's prison if he didn't make us laugh. Even Seth Rogen gets girls. And it's not because of his hair gel. Figure out what makes her squirt Diet Coke through her nose and she's yours—so long as you also bathe regularly and are not on a poster at the courthouse. A note of caution here: Humor is always subjective, and requires an element of surprise. Therefore repeating the same jokes you used on your first date—whether that was fourteen years ago or four days ago—will not earn her favor. In fact, the lack of new jokes may be the sole reason many men resort to womanizing. It's not that they can't get enough variety in women; they can't get enough variety in their routines. Instead of coming up with new material, they cycle through chicks instead. But that's just lazy. Let's make a deal, once

we've heard your greatest hits, ten, twenty, a hundred times—
you come up with some new lines, and we'll promise to laugh.

6. Groping is not sexy.

Most single men wouldn't think of reaching out for an
uninvited squeeze. (Okay, they'd think of it, but they wouldn't
do it.) Yet, once in a committed relationship, some men treat
a woman like a chew toy, pouncing and drooling over her at
the slightest provocation. Most women do not respond well
to ass grabs and "accidental" breast grazing. Those of us with
young children have probably been climbed and pulled upon
all day. And older girls have things going on in places you
are better to keep your hands out of until you get the all clear.
Don't get me wrong. There is a time and a place for man-
handling, desk-clearing, take-me-now moves. It may or may
not be while she is bent over the dishwasher. You will know.
If you need help, study Mickey Rourke's movies. That guy is
hideous and yet he still closes the deal. Every time. (Which
would not be the case if women were the visual ones.)

7. Cuddling is not optional.

We are not trying to annoy and smother you with our
incessant requests for physical closeness, after the other
physical closeness. It's this blasted biology kicking in again.
A woman's need to cuddle is chemical, especially but not
limited to the minutes just after sex. The Oxytocin released
during sex makes us like you better and want to snuggle up.
Do not be afraid; it doesn't last long. You will soon be watching the game or snoring or eating something with cheese
and grease. In addition to the post-coital tolerance of close-

ness, you might also try some non-sexual physical affection at any time, just because. Cuddles have been known to lead to groping, and if that happens then I commend you. But you might be shocked to learn how far a simple hug will get you when the recipient knows your gesture is not a direct play for sex. (Indirect plays work so much better.)

8. We don't actually need you.

Don't be discouraged. We don't need you, but we do want you, and that's so much better. This may be a difficult truth for men who were brought up to be providers, to take on the hard labor of family life, to be depended on financially and physically. But women are no longer traded to the highest bidder by their fathers or expected to subsume their every aspiration to the yoke of motherhood. For millennia we belonged to you, just because. Not so much anymore. Women are graduating college at higher rates than men, and soon— God-willing—we will be paid accordingly for the same work we do. We can buy our own homes and hire out the heavy lifting. We have amazing friendships with other women to feed our need for emotional connection. And we have rechargeable Energizers for guaranteed orgasms. If we are with you—and we are—it's not because we need to be. When you wake up to our shining (or not so shining) faces, then you know that despite all other alternatives, we really, truly want to be with you.

9. We like words.

So cliché, and yet so true. We're women. We talk. We talk it up, we talk it over, we talk it out. That's why we have all those girlfriends. However, other women are not always available. Sometimes we actually need to talk to you. (Fine, we need you a little.) But unless we specifically ask you to solve our problems, we usually do not want you to offer solutions. We prefer that you listen, empathize, nod, agree, and give us a hug. That is not to say we don't want to hear from you. Tell a woman she is beautiful (or hot or sexy or however she likes to hear it). Tell her this when she looks great and when she feels terrible. If she balks and turns away and worries that you don't mean it, take her by the shoulders, look into her eyes, and assure her that you do. Tell her she is great at her job, whether that job involves pre-dawn flights and endless sales meetings or feeding small humans and cleaning their waste. Tell her there is no one else you would rather be with. Mean it. In fact, any time something sweet pops into your head, let it out. Tell her all those things you think but too often keep to yourself.

10. We do not want honesty.

Don't get excited, you're not allowed to lie. We need the truth in regard to all things that can be measured and verified—things like legal documents you have signed and whether or not there were any women present at the hunting lodge. Feelings, however, fall into a different category. We don't really want to know if you're not quite ready to commit, that you once pined for one of our friends, or that you like to watch the new neighbor roll her trash can to the curb. All we really want to know is that you must have us, all of us, and nothing but us— exclusively and unceasingly—for now and evermore. If you can't fake that, what do you bring to the table? If a woman is mature, confident, and kind enough to tell you exactly what she needs to hear, just say it. (We like words, remember?) And don't complain if she asks for something completely different tomorrow. Be grateful that she values you enough to help you meet her needs.

Bottom line: We're not as complicated as you think. You're simple, we both know that. But so are we. We just want to be appreciated, emotionally, intellectually, and physically. Be generous with compliments and physical affection. In return, we will occasionally tell you that you are right. Maybe. And perhaps someday we'll find that G-Spot. Together.

The Other Woman: Henrietta

MOVING MAKES ME A TEENY TINY bit crazy. The last
time I had to suffer the anxiety attack that is moving was,
thankfully, nearly ten years ago. We were relocating from
Texas to Arkansas, where my husband had taken a new job.
He'd already been working in our new town for a couple of
months before the kids and I followed. Once there, my days
consisted of caring for two young children, unpacking, and
trying to make our new house into a home. I was looking for
a key in my husband's coat pocket one day when I found a
map. Written there, over the neat grid of streets was a single
word.

Henrietta.

I started to hyperventilate and my hands and gut filled
with a shot of panic. I almost threw up, right there in the
coat closet.

Henrietta.

Dramatic scenes from the *Lifetime* channel played in my
imagination. Two months alone was all it had taken for my

husband to find some Arkansas skank. Soon he'd leave the kids and me to live with this Walmart greeter in her trailer out on Highway 102. My imagination works fast on adrenaline.

Breathe, I told myself. Keep calm. I wanted to dial his number immediately, but I had to be smart. You need evidence for this kind of thing. I went through the rest of the pockets. The only offense I could document was a Big Mac at lunch. Surely, there had to be some damning confirmation that would prove inconclusively that my husband of a decade was trading down.

Henrietta.

That bitch. I continued to search—his pants, the little basket he keeps in the closet, the tool drawer. Nothing. Oh, sure, he'd learned to cover his tracks. How quickly he'd become so skilled at infidelity. Or had he been deceiving me all along? Bastard. Still, something wasn't quite right. Wasn't I supposed to have some kind of feeling about this? Wouldn't I know if he were cheating on me? To hell with instincts. I could not deny the facts there in his unattractive scrawl:

Henrietta.

By the time he got home that night, I had still not discovered any adulterous data. I played it cool, waiting until we were alone. I handed him the map.

"I found this in your pocket."

He took it. "Yeah?"

I raised my eyebrows, giving him ample opportunity for a full confession, unprompted. He said nothing, and set the map on the counter.

"Who is Henrietta?" I asked.

"Who?"

I looked at the map. "Henrietta." I picked it up and unfolded it, tapping the incriminating name. "There. Henrietta."

He looked at the map, then at me, and back to the map.

"So, let me get this straight," he said. "You think I'm having an affair—with a woman named Henrietta?"

Had he been angry, it would have been just like the scene in the imaginary *Lifetime* movie. But he wasn't. He was laughing.

"Um," I said. "Yes?"

"Seriously?"

I shrugged.

"You don't think I could do better than 'Henrietta'?" He shook his head. I wavered, but still.

Henrietta!

"It's the title company."

Oh, puhleeeze. "I think I would have remembered a *Henrietta* at the title company."

"This is a map." He picked it up. "The office was on Henrietta Street. Remember?"

Oh...

"Sorry?"

Henrietta has become our running joke. About my healthy fantasy life, and his poor taste in mistresses. At this point he could have the name tattooed on his thigh and I wouldn't think he was cheating. Guaranteed laughs, sure. But I'm screwed if he actually meets a hot chick named Henrietta.

The Seventeen-Year Itch

AN ACQUAINTANCE OF MINE SHOWED off her new engagement ring at the Junior League meeting. Her diamond was bigger than my car and by my quick calculations cost more than my house. The stone was so big that when she first saw it, my friend did not think it could be real. Or maybe she just couldn't believe this ring, any ring, wasn't a mirage. She had been "dating" her new fiancé for seventeen years. This man has taken her to the top of the Eiffel Tower, where a proposal was as certain as croissants in the morning and wine at noon. However, no knee was dropped. He let her down then, and on many other similarly romantic occasions, but when he finally offered a contract, the bling did not disappoint.

Color me envious of the trips, the freedom, and all that compressed carbon. But mostly I'm curious. What does a seventeen-year courtship feel like? My husband and I have been married longer than that. And it shows. Some days more than others, like today when my twelve-year-old daughter chastised us for discussing the specifics of not only our dog's diarrhea, but also our own. True love, right there. That's what you get after two decades of sharing the same sheets—if you're lucky.

Even in the best marriages where both parties enjoy one another's company, laugh at each other's jokes, and achieve a healthy and mutually agreeable number of orgasms, it's still marriage, and marriage is the hardest thing. That's why there are legal documents. And the best outcome is death. Lifetime commitment can be freeing, or it can make you question the value of living in a world forever bereft of true love's first kiss. Ecstasy is all about firsts. Ask any drug addict.

Of course, relationships progress whether or not there is a ring and a contract. I suspect seventeen years worth of dirty underwear and misplaced keys are just as irritating to the unmarried as the lawfully wedded. But there is something different when you sign the license. There just is.

Back to diamonds.

Mine is beautiful. It's a carat. But compared to my friend's rock, it looked like a promise ring given on the broken step of a trailer down by the river. I took a picture of my hand and my diamond next to my friend's hand and her diamond and sent the image to my husband.

I included a message: *Step it up*.

No response. What was his problem? Clearly, my text was hilarious and playful. Didn't he get me? Was his manhood really so fragile? But he was out with some guys from work at one of those places where the waitresses wear cutoff shorts, cowboy boots, and tops made out of tube socks. The thought of them made me wonder if I was the one who needed to step it up. After a few minutes I tried again.

Hello?

Nothing.

At home I interrogated him. Why didn't he answer? It could have been an emergency. More important, it could have been a sext.

"You texted me?"

Nice try.

"Of course I did. Don't you know how to use your phone?"

He sighed. He does that a lot. You probably would too after seventeen years married to me. Then he admitted that yeah, okay, he knew there was a text but how was he supposed to see a picture that small? I showed him how to make it larger.

"But I sent you a message too. Can't you see those?"

And then the real truth—the seventeen-year truth, the midlife truth—came out. My husband could not bear to break out the reading glasses in front of the bandana-clad waitress.

My friend's new ring may reflect more light, but I've had mine longer. I've had it since my husband could see its diamond without his readers.

Who Peed on My Yoga Mat?

The Best $17 He Ever Spent

THE SUMMER OF 2011 WAS EXPENSIVE. There was the once-in-a-lifetime European vacation, my son's aerospace engineering camp, and an unexplained increase in my pedicure fees. My husband and I also celebrated our seventeenth wedding anniversary. Not a milestone year as anniversaries go, but a big number anyway. It would have been nice to spend accordingly. If only my fingers weren't full of paper cuts from the credit card statements.

It never matters what we spend though, right? It's all symbolic. Still, there could be some resentment if one were to receive, say a bunch of grocery store daisies and the other received a watch of the behind-the-counter variety. We needed ground rules. I suggested a spending limit, based on current finances. So, after much deliberation, to mark seventeen years of marriage, we agreed to spend no more than seventeen dollars each.

What the hell was I thinking?

As the day neared I still had no ideas for a suitable

seventeen-dollar gift. At dinner with my girlfriends, drinking champagne and spending much more than seventeen dollars, I threw out a ridiculous idea. The joke was met with wild enthusiasm.

"Oh, you HAVE to do that!"

"Yes, you do! That would be AWESOME!"

"Hilarious!"

I had no intention of following through, but as the evening wore on the joke kept coming back around. The more I heard it, the more wine I drank, the better it sounded.

"When is your anniversary?" a friend asked.

"Tomorrow."

"That's it. You're doing it," my friend said. "What other choice do you have?"

She was right. My idea was fun, clever, and most important—the only one I had.

Later, at home, I worked up a game plan and ran through a trial run in my closet. I could totally do this.

The next day, our anniversary, my husband took the kids out to find something—anything—for me. I rested smug in the knowledge that my gift was under control. The only catch was that the kids really wanted to know what I was getting Daddy for our anniversary, and I couldn't tell them.

"I won't tell. I promise!" said the little one.

"C'mon, Mom," my son said. "What's the big secret?"

When it was time to deliver, I told the kids to find something to watch on TV. I set things up so that when my husband came into the bedroom he found my iPhone in the dock and cued to Pandora's Roxy Music channel, candles on the nightstand, and an envelope on the bed.

Inside: Seventeen ones and a note that read, *Make it rain, Babe.*

Oh, yeah. Jackpot wife. Right? Except that my closet dress rehearsal had not fully prepared me for what to do next. Alcohol seemed a good idea. John opened the wine that was my anniversary gift from him, our honeymoon wine, Chateau St. Michele, a Reisling because we married young. Two glasses later it was time to put out. There was some awkward negotiation to begin the dance. You see, while I was fairly comfortable putting on a show, I wasn't quite sure where the cash came in.

He pulled out the money, the ones. "How much will three dollars get me?"

The humiliation was pretend, and still palpable. "We have to pretend those are twenties," I said. "At least."

That didn't help. Stripping is easy; translating it into cash takes skill. However, I'd committed and now I had to deliver, at least seventeen dollars' worth. I am a woman of principles, after all. I continued the bump and grind, calling on all my natural and unnatural talents. I even stopped every now and then to extract more cash from the pocket where John was keeping his ones. It wasn't pretty, but at least these less-than-smooth interruptions were expected. The real mood killer was when the sultry sounds of Bryan Ferry were interrupted with a Staples commercial.

If only there were an Easy Button for anniversaries.

This year's celebration was certainly memorable, inexpensive, and had a happy ending. Especially since I got my seventeen dollars back.

LELA DAVIDSON

Sexy Things My Husband Won't Do

I DON'T ENVY MY SINGLE FRIENDS. But I do like to go dancing with the girls. We hit the clubs in cute dresses, fabulous shoes, and in my case—more eyeliner than the members of every 80s hair band combined. The door boys let us in under the Cougar Clause, and we plan to work this trend until its bitter Botox end. I like the loud music, the drinking, and the dancing, but I wouldn't trade my domestic bliss for The Scene. It is not pretty out there.

On a recent Girls' Night Out in Tulsa, my friends and I started the evening at a wine bar. (Translation: Comfortable seating, 35-55 years old, conservative attire.) No sooner had we claimed our overstuffed real estate than a boisterous gentleman we'll call Bob greeted us. Bob was so intent on making sure the six of us ladies had a good time that at first we assumed he was the proprietor, or maybe an especially fulfilled employee. However, when Bob failed to take our drink order, suggested we call him Big Bob, and embarked on an extended reminiscence of his high school basketball career, it became clear we were on our own for drinks. Amid Bob's gregarious tale telling we sent a scout to the bar. When she tried to hand her credit card to the bartender, Bob intervened. He wanted to cover our round. Back on the couches much fuss was made over Bob's generous contribution and soon we were sipping and chatting about other things.

At the same time, two more women arrived and joined our group. It was getting cozy on those sofas, and on one of his showy trips to the bar to fetch drinks, Bob's seat was taken. Instead of gallantly standing by, continuing to enjoy our company (including those of us who were also standing or less-than-comfortably perched on bookshelves), Bob asked one of us to get up so he could have her seat.

"You can sit on my lap!"

Um… no.

Men: You don't have to be young to get our attention. You don't have to be rich. You don't have to be sexy. We appreciate conversation and appreciation. Even boring stories and the ill-advised hand on the leg we can accept, so long as you are entertaining us.

But don't push it.

"I just bought you drinks and you won't even sit on my lap?" Bob said. "That's not very professional."

Dear, sweet, pathetic Bob. Perhaps if you're looking for a professional, you hit the wrong bar.

Another time, I was with two other forty-somethings, looking for excitement at midnight in Oklahoma City. (I know. You're jealous. Try to control yourself.) As the Embassy Suites bartender locked up the liquor and wiped down the counter one last time, he told us to hit Club Rodeo.

"There's bull riding," he said. You know what I pictured immediately, right? Dolly Parton and John Travolta, mechanical bull, starched Wranglers, and shirts with shiny snaps. Why not? I'm nothing if not adventurous. When in Oklahoma, and all.

The six-dollar cover charge fostered high expectations, which were only enhanced by the stench of manure that hit us as we walked in the front door. Appropriate, if not a bit over-the-top. The huge dance floor with all those decades-younger-than-us people moving in synchronized steps mesmerized me. The music spanned multiple genres from Brad Paisley to Eminem to Michael Jackson, with assorted styles of twenty-two year olds to match. Before I fully absorbed the diversity of the crowd, I heard a familiar tune. It was the hockey rumble remix, and it blared as the people dispersed, revealing a most unexpected sight. There, just past the sticky spot where a lanky kid in a cowboy hat had just executed a flawless moonwalk, was a live bull. The puny gates holding it back did not instill confidence. This is when I decided we would not be drinking. All wits would be about us in this fine establishment. As authentic looking guys with numbers pinned to their chests lined up on hay bales, I recalled the bartender's parting words.

There's bull riding.

Oh... *that's* what he meant.

Eight seconds passes quickly. Soon we were back to the dancing. Without certain rap video moves—not to mention a Rohypnol buzz—my companions and I were not sought after dance partners.

"I think we're doing this wrong," one of them said.

"Actually, I think we're good." Any differently and we would have needed lawyers and antibiotics. Instead, we only required moderate chiropractic adjustments.

The club environment certainly explains the popularity of online dating. I have friends with profiles on three, four, five different sites. And I am fascinated. The last time I was on the market, you had to do things the old-fashioned way, face-to-face with lip gloss and cheap beer. There was no easy weed-out mechanism. You couldn't multitask a first date while simultaneously finishing up a sales presentation and watching The Bachelor on DVR. (Okay, I'm exaggerating. Nobody worth dating watches The Bachelor.) But as wonderful as it may seem, all the technology does not make my single friends any more successful at coupling up. I understand the appeal of databases that find the ideal mate. However, like unicorns and fat-free pizza, I don't believe such things exist.

Mates are mates. Forget the soul business; Reese Witherspoon movies be damned. I asked my husband recently if he thought an online dating service would have worked for us. Because I don't. I doubt any man-made algorithm would have put us together, which may account for why we are still together. My 20-year companion looked at me and sighed. "Did the internet even exist when we met?"

"No," I said. "But we did have Match.com. It was called a bar."

I met my husband over a dollar-pitcher of private label beer. God bless Speedy O'Tubbs. It was simple back then.

And we were babies. I wouldn't want to be dating now, at this age, in this time. My friends are older, wiser. They have the Internet and checklists. I don't know how they do it. I hear stories of grandfathers who still live with their mothers and women running credit reports before the first date. My friends must factor in exes, custody schedules, and the new math required to determine how many dates until you can finally strip down and get what you came for. Which leads me to the real reason I'd never leave my husband for the modern dating game: Bikini area maintenance. Brazilian, American, French. The standards are too high for over-achieving Playmates-of-the-Month, much less over-40 play date facilitators.

Still, I enjoy living vicariously through my dating friends. Closer to home, the boys are more subtle. Southern gentlemen, if you will. Especially the undergrads on our favorite local dance floor.

"Hey, what are you doing after this?" a young one asked me recently.

After this? What is he talking about? There is no after this. This IS this.

His question reminded me to check the time because *this* needed to end in forty-five minutes—before the taxi fare doubled. I hated to disappoint, so instead of explaining why I need to leave so early, as well as the raging "after party" that is my facial cleansing routine, I told him we were there to celebrate my friend's impending nuptials.

"Why don't you give me your phone number?"

So much for small talk.

"You know what," I said "I'm married, so you probably don't want my number."

"Married, huh?" He pondered a moment. "Give me your number. I'll do everything your husband won't do."

Really? Everything my husband won't do?

Everything?

Was this young man actually offering to wash windows and grout, stop for directions, clean the crumbs around the toaster, endure the entire series of *Twilight* movies, and use the last of the mustard before opening a new bottle?

Jackpot!

Who says you can't meet quality men in a club? I may have misjudged this whole new dating world. Could I really trade my husband in for one of these do-it-all men? And are there women out there willing to play out his every fantasy? Such as not stabbing him with their toenails, actually enjoying *The Matrix* on the eighth viewing, and sitting with him for long stretches without speaking? Sometimes I wonder if we have both missed many, many exciting opportunities.

And then I remember Bob, and I shine up my wedding band.

ACKNOWLEDGEMENTS

❧

ONE THING I'VE LEARNED since publishing my first book was that it is impossible to thank everyone who contributes to the creation and success any book. There are many pieces to my writing life that blend and meld. It is impossible to parse out the efforts of this book from the whole that is my writing career.

First, I thank my readers, which sounds more than a little pretentious. I have been amazed and humbled by the success of my first book, *Blacklisted from the PTA*. I appreciate each of you who have purchased, read, shared, and talked about my work with your friends, sisters, moms, and daughters. Thank you for every blog post and social media shout out. Without your support and encouragement, this book would not exist. I will keep telling our stories as long as you're willing to listen.

Thanks to the close circle of friends who have been so involved in helping to launch this book and boost my confidence: Lori Bremer, Kelley Emeterio, Lori Walker, Tina Winham and Gracie Ziegler.

Thank you, Rebecca Dube and Kavita White, my editors at TODAY Moms, who always encourage me to write with voice and stretch beyond my comfort zone. Thanks to Kelly

Wallace, Sharon Rowley, and all the editors at iVillage for welcoming me to the team. Thanks to Christina Katz, who continues to be a valuable mentor and trusted friend. I could not do it without the support of Patricia Smith, my thorough and insightful editor. Thanks to Nancy Cleary, for excellent cover design and guidance. And thanks to Tom Barczak and Eric Reitan for help with Amazon.com and men's Facebook posts.

Thanks to Tracy Beckerman, Jenna McCarthy, Diane Mizota, Robin O'Bryant, Kyran Pittman, Eric Ruhalter, and Rob Sachs for your early support and kind words.

I thank my children, who still let me share some things about them, even now that they are teenagers. And to their friends, who occasionally try to convince them that I am cool. Which I am not. Without my kids, most of the stories I tell would never have happened to me. My utmost gratitude goes to my husband, John, who did not know he was signing on to have the details of our marital life chronicled for public consumption.

I am—in short—the luckiest girl I know. Thanks for reading.